Bloom's

GUIDES

George Orwell's
Animal Farm

The Adventures of Huckleberry Finn
All the Pretty Horses
Animal Farm
Beloved
Brave New World
The Chosen
The Crucible
Cry, the Beloved Country
Death of a Salesman
The Grapes of Wrath
Great Expectations
The Great Gatsby
Hamlet
The Handmaid's Tale
The House on Mango Street
I Know Why the Caged Bird Sings
The Iliad
Lord of the Flies
Macbeth
Maggie: A Girl of the Streets
The Member of the Wedding
Of Mice and Men
1984
One Hundred Years of Solitude
Pride and Prejudice
Ragtime
Romeo and Juliet
The Scarlet Letter
Snow Falling on Cedars
A Streetcar Named Desire
The Things They Carried
To Kill a Mockingbird

Bloom's
GUIDES

George Orwell's
Animal Farm

Edited & with an Introduction
by Harold Bloom

CHELSEA HOUSE
PUBLISHERS
An imprint of Infobase Publishing

Bloom's Guides: Animal Farm

Copyright © 2006 by Infobase Publishing
Introduction © 2006 by Harold Bloom

Chelsea House
An imprint of Infobase Publishing
132 West 31st Street
New York NY 10001

Library of Congress Cataloging-in-Publication Data
George Orwell's Animal Farm / Harold Bloom, ed.
   p. cm. — (Bloom's guides)
  Includes bibliographical references and index.
  ISBN 0-7910-8583-X
 1. Orwell, George, 1903-1950. Animal farm. 2. Animals in literature.
3. Social problems in literature. 4. Political fiction, English—
History and criticism. 5. Satire, English—History and criticism.
6. Fables, English—History and criticism. I. Title: Animal Farm.
II. Bloom, Harold. III. Series.
  PR6029.R8A63 2006
  823'.912—dc22   2005038035

Contributing Editor: Sarah Robbins
Cover design by Takeshi Takahashi

Printed in the United States of America

Bang EJB 10 9 8 7 6 5 4 3 2 1

This book is printed on acid-free paper.

Contents

Introduction

HAROLD BLOOM

One critic remarked of George Orwell that he wrote sympathetically about human beings only when he presented them as animals. The truth of this can be tested by comparing *Animal Farm* to *Nineteen Eighty-Four;* Napoleon (Stalin) is preferable to the torturer O'Brien, perhaps because even a whip-wielding boar is more tolerated by Orwell than a sadistic human. Poor Boxer, the martyred workhorse, is certainly more lovable than Winston Smith, and Mollie the flirtatious mare is more charming than poor Julia. Orwell's dislike of people resembles that of a much greater moral satirist, Jonathan Swift: Each loved individual persons, while despising mankind in the mass. Whatever the aesthetic flaws of *Animal Farm*, it seems to me a better book than *Nineteen Eighty-Four*, primarily because it allows us a few animals with whom we can identify. Even Benjamin, the ill-tempered old donkey, silent and cynical, and incapable of laughing, still becomes somewhat dear to us, largely because of his devotion to the heroic Boxer. I'm not certain that I don't prefer Snowball (Trotsky) to anyone at all in *Nineteen Eighty-Four*, because at least he is vivacious and inventive.

The great Canadian critic Northrop Frye observed that *Animal Farm* adapts from Swift's *A Tale of a Tub* the classical formula of much literary satire: "the corruption of principle by expediency," or the fall of Utopia. Unlike Swift, however, as Frye again notes, Orwell is not concerned with motivation. The reader is not encouraged to ask: What does the inscrutable Napoleon-Stalin want? Orwell's point may be that absolute power is desired by tyrants simply for its own sake, but *Animal Farm* hardly makes that very clear. The beast-fable is a fascinating genre, but it demands a certain psychological clarity, whether in Chaucer or in Thurber, and *Animal Farm* mostly evades psychological categories.

Orwell essentially was a liberal moralist, grimly preoccupied with preserving a few old-fashioned virtues while fearing that the technological future would only enhance human depravity. *Animal Farm*, like *Nineteen Eighty-Four*, retains its relevance because we are entering into a computerized world where a post-Orwellian "virtual reality" could be used as yet another betrayal of individual liberty. Part of the residual strength of *Animal Farm* is that we can imagine a version of it in early twenty-first century America in which all the "animals" will be compelled to live some variant upon a theocratic "Contract with the American Family." Perhaps the motto of that theocracy will be: "All animals are holy, but some animals are holier than others."

Biographical Sketch

George Orwell was born Eric Arthur Blair in Motihari, Bengal, India, on June 25, 1903, to Richard Blair, an opium agent in the Indian Civil Service, and Ida Mabel Blair. A year later, Orwell, his mother, and his sister Marjorie returned to England and settled in the Oxfordshire town of Henley-on-Thames; Richard remained in India to monitor what was then a lucrative business, returning home only once, in 1907. Orwell's stint at the prep school St. Cyprian's, where he met the writer Cyril Connolly, later inspired the autobiographical essay "Such, Such Were the Joys," which is a riff on the William Blake piece from *Songs of Innocence* and a tale of abuses by fellow students and the schoolmistress. He visited home and family—which now included his younger sister, Avril, who probably was conceived during Richard's one visit—in the country on the Thames. Then in 1917, just before the October Revolution, in Russia, he was enrolled in the prestigious Eton as a King's Scholar. There he read voraciously—favoring Jack London, George Bernard Shaw, and H.G. Wells—enrolled in the school's Officer's Training Corps, and first became aware of British society's class prejudice. When he missed his train on the way back from an Officer's Training weekend, he was forced to spend the night in Plymouth, sleeping on the ground and foraging for food. This experience of tramping fascinated him and inspired a longstanding practice that would later take him to London and Paris and inspire his first published work.

When Orwell failed to win a university scholarship, and when his father—now retired—refused to pay for college, he became a British officer of the Indian Imperial Police in Burma, where his mother still had relatives. In the early 1920s, a strong Burmese nationalist movement was rebelling against British colonial authorities. This civil unrest, in addition to the class distinctions, enslaved every level of Burmese society. Gang violence and crime riddled the area. Orwell was nineteen when he arrived, and he stayed for five years. There he had experiences that would later inspire such works as "A Hanging" and "Shooting an Elephant." Guilt-ridden and disgusted by the murders he had seen, he later wrote about his experiences in *Burmese Days*: "The landscapes of Burma, which, when I was among them, so appalled me as to assume the qualities of nightmare, afterwards stayed so hauntingly in my mind that I was obliged to write a novel about them to get rid of them." He left the service in 1927 and rededicated his energy to writing. "Between the ages of about seventeen and twenty-four I tried to abandon [the idea of writing]," he wrote later, "but I did this with the consciousness that I was outraging my true nature and that sooner or later I should have to settle down and write books."

Orwell moved to London and found lodging in an inexpensive boarding house, though he spent many of his nights in the poverty-stricken East End in order to gain an understanding of those he had ruled over for years. He moved to Paris and traveled similarly there—though he was too late for the golden days experienced by expatriates such as Hemingway, Fitzgerald, and others, he was inspired by his proximity to the Pantheon (the final resting place of greats from Voltaire to Zola). Though he did publish a bit, he soon ran out of money and was forced to pawn his overcoat and find a job as a dishwasher. He had always suffered from lung problems, and when he was stricken with pneumonia, he returned to his parents' home in Southwold where he completed the manuscript for *Down and Out in Paris and London*. After a number of publishers' rejections, Victor Gollancz agreed to publish it; he did so in 1933, under the pseudonym George Orwell. A success at age 30, Orwell immediately got started on *Burmese Days*, his first novel, and in the meantime he taught school and took a job in a bookstore—Booklovers' Corner, which later became the subject of the essay "Bookshop Memories."

Orwell wrote that he was particularly influenced by Somerset Maugham and his notion of writing from experience. *Burmese Days*, published in 1934, is based in a place like Katha, his last post in Burma, and is strongly influenced by E.M. Forster's *A Passage to India*. Rayner Heppenstall, one of

Orwell's colleagues at the *Adelphi*, introduced him to Eileen Maud O'Shaughnessy, a graduate student in educational psychology. The day after they met, Orwell described her to a friend by saying: "Now that's the type of girl I'd like to marry!" They did so on June 9, 1936. After writing his third novel, *Keep the Aspidistra Flying*—about which he later said, "it is invariably where I lacked a political purpose that I wrote lifeless books"— his publisher asked him if he would write a book about unemployment and the living conditions in northern England. So Orwell spent the winter of 1936 traveling amid industrial districts, gathering material for *The Road to Wigan Pier*. This experience pushed him closer to socialism, as he thought the contrast between rich and poor horrifying. Critics compare that work, which was published in 1937, to the likes of Carlyle's "Chartism," Engels' *The Condition of the Working Class in England in 1844*, and Charles Dickens' *Hard Times*.

After the outbreak of the Spanish Civil War, Orwell and Eileen traveled overseas to work for the antifascist movement, which, he later wrote in *Homage to Catalonia*, was "at that time and in that atmosphere ... the only conceivable thing to do." Upon his arrival in Barcelona he reported to the headquarters of POUM, the Unified Marxist Workers' Party. The anarchists occupied Catalonia, and Orwell, stationed in the trenches with the Loyalists, scribbled notes and sent them to Eileen, who was serving as a secretary for the Independent Labour Party. To Orwell's amazement, Stalin's purge of the Communist party, which had begun in 1934, had spread to Western Europe— POUM was being hunted down by the Soviet police, and Spanish communists began searching through the couple's things. In May 1936 an enemy bullet hit Orwell in the throat, narrowly missing his carotid artery. While he was recovering, he and his wife were forced to flee when they were accused of treason.

The six months spent in Spain had a profound effect on Orwell's career. In "Why I Write" he says, "Every line of work that I have written since 1936 has been written, directly or indirectly, against totalitarianism and for democratic Socialism.... What I have most wanted to do throughout the past ten years is to make political writing into an art. My starting point is always a feeling of partisanship, a sense of injustice." Upon his return, he became frustrated by the British liberal press' lack of attention to the atrocities. *Homage to Catalonia*, the self-proclaimed "best book I have written," was published in 1938, though not without struggle—Gollancz rejected it before he even read it. Orwell began to write editorials and book reviews for *The Pioneer*. When he began losing weight and spitting up blood, the diagnosis was tuberculosis. He visited his dying father and wrote *Coming Up for Air*.

When WWII broke out, Orwell and Eileen returned to London, where Eileen got a job overseeing a government program called "The Kitchen Front," which espoused the virtues of rationing, and Orwell joined the civilian militia. He also reviewed films for *Time and Tide* and wrote two books of criticism, *Inside the Whale* and *The Lion and the Unicorn*, the latter which offered socialistic solutions to wartime problems. He befriended Arthur Koestler, who wrote *Darkness at Noon*, about the psychological effects of the Moscow Purge Trials. He and Eileen survived the Blitz, though one day, the force of a "doodle bug" explosion knocked down the walls of their flat. In August 1941 Orwell began working at the BBC, and the censorship and propaganda there, which discouraged him so profoundly, became a model for *1984*. He resigned in September 1943 and became literary editor of the *Tribune* while beginning work on *Animal Farm*. He discussed every detail of the book with Eileen and completed it in 1944—that same year, they adopted a son, Richard. Despite the publication struggles the book was released in August 1945 to high acclaim. Though Orwell only received a small advance for it, it was accepted by the American Book-of-the-Month Club and sold more than 600,000 copies in the United States alone.

In 1945 Orwell became a war correspondent for the *Observer* and the *Manchester Evening News*, and he traveled through Europe, where he met Hemingway (who called *Homage to Catalonia* a first-rate book and said that their politics were close and that he regretted that Orwell fought for POUM and not the International Brigades). While Orwell was overseas working, Eileen died of heart failure during a hysterectomy. This news took him by surprise, as he'd only learned of her condition at the last minute. As he was grieving, *Animal Farm* was published, and he continued to seek refuge in his work, publishing more than 130 articles and reviews in the next year. Success tired Orwell, however, and he began escaping to the Scottish island of Jura with Richard so that he could focus on literature and politics. He continued publishing essays—those on Swift, Dickens, Kipling, and Henry Miller are considered essentials. His plans to travel abroad were thwarted by another relapse in late 1947, which resulted in a pneumothorax operation. He proposed marriage to several young women, emphasizing his poor health, and began work on *Nineteen Eighty-Four*, explaining to friends that he couldn't focus on his health until he'd finished his book. *Nineteen Eighty-Four*'s grim predictions for the future created controversy, but it garnered praise from the likes of Aldous Huxley, Lionel Trilling, and Czeslaw Milosz. After he finished it he entered the Cotswold Sanatorium near Gloucester, where he was visited by Sonia Brownell—Cyril Connolly's former editorial assistant, whom he had met years earlier and who was the inspiration for the character of Julia in *Nineteen Eighty-Four*. They were married in 1949, and when Orwell died in January 1950, at age 46, he left his entire estate to her and none to his son, Richard, who was raised by Orwell's sister, Avril. Only after Sonia's death in 1980 did Richard inherit his father's estate.

The Story Behind the Story

Though *Animal Farm* was published in 1945, the idea for the work germinated during the dwindling days of the Spanish Civil War. "Having barely escaped from the long reach of Stalin's agents," explains biographer Michael Shelden, "[Orwell] began to reflect on how a genuine revolutionary movement in Spain could have allowed itself to come so completely under the control of a dictator living thousands of miles away." Orwell thought the Russian Communists had betrayed the socialist ideals set out by Marx and Engels, and he felt that Western allegiance to Russia was obscuring the hypocrisy of the Stalinist regime. He began working on the manuscript in London in 1943, while he was serving as literary editor of the socialist weekly the *Tribune*, and finished the manuscript a scant four months later, in February 1944, while he and his wife, Eileen, were living in London under constant threat of air raids. He shared a good deal of the story with Eileen, often reading entire passages aloud for her approval, and he modeled some of his animal "characters" on his own animals—his donkeys in Burma, and the chickens and goats that he and Eileen had raised. Despite the childlike notion of animals as protagonists, the work's aim was clear from the introduction, in which Orwell writes: "Nothing has contributed so much to the corruption of the original idea of Socialism as the belief that Russia is a Socialist country and that every act of its rulers must be excused.... For the past ten years I have been convinced that the destruction of the Soviet myth was essential if we wanted a revival of the Socialist movement." The month of the book's completion, one of his articles in the *Observer* insisted that "the Spanish war [should] be kept always in mind as an object-lesson in the folly and meanness of Power Politics." Though Orwell was certain that the time had come to address such corruption, his stance was not entirely welcome in a world still wracked by suspicion and political unrest.

In Britain, the manuscript was rejected by five publishers, including T.S. Eliot, who was at the time one of the editorial directors at Faber & Faber. After complimenting Orwell by comparing his work to that of Swift, Eliot said he'd found the fable negative and Trotskyist and suggested that the views espoused did not fit the time. "'After all,'" he wrote, "'your pigs are far more intellectual than the other animals, and therefore the best qualified to run the farm—in fact, there couldn't have been an Animal Farm at all without them: so that what was needed (some might argue), was not more communism but more public-spirited pigs.'"[1] In America, twenty publishers rejected it. Some claimed they were not equipped to produce the book because of a wartime paper shortage, but the truth was that Stalin had recently aligned himself with Britain, which distracted public consciousness from the horror of Stalin's purges. *Animal Farm* was finally published by Secker and Warburg in August 1945, the same month as the atomic bombing of Hiroshima. Roosevelt had recently died, Mussolini had been killed, and Hitler had committed suicide. In the aftermath of war, the book sold more than 25,000 hardcover copies in the first five years. And the American version, which appeared in 1946, sold 590,000 in four years. It was later translated into 32 languages.

All of its early criticism was completely colored by the reviewers' opinion of Stalinist Russia. Nevertheless, this was the book that earned him acclaim. He earned the lead review in *The New Yorker*, and Edmund Wilson called the book "absolutely first-rate" and compared Orwell to Voltaire and Swift. Graham Greene lauded Orwell's bravery for making a strong statement during a time of war; he took *Animal Farm*'s publication as a sign of peace: "Writers may pass, like everyone else, through the opium dream of Munich and Yalta, but no literature comes out of that dream. Literature is concerned above everything else with the accurate expression of a personal vision, while appeasement is a matter of compromise." Spencer Brown said, "No other writer has shown us so clearly the worst tragedy of our age."

Since Orwell's fable was straightforward enough to be subject to interpretation, the Right used his book as a tool of propaganda, to prove that revolutions were doomed to failure.

According to Frances Stonor Saunders, after Orwell's death the CIA bought the film rights to *Animal Farm* and had an animated film produced in Britain. The book's final scene was left out. In the new ending, the animals storm the farmhouse and take it back from the pigs. This type of propaganda certainly would not have pleased Orwell, who once worked as a propagandist for the BBC; critics C. Fleay and M.L. Sanders have suggested that *Animal Farm* "was a particular reaction to his BBC experience and that in one sense it was a work of atonement."

Note

1. T.S. Eliot, letter to Orwell, 13 July 1944 in *The Times*, 6 January 1969, p.9.

List of Characters

"A large, rather fierce-looking Berkshire boar, the only Berkshire on the farm, not much of a talker, but with a reputation for getting his own way," **Napoleon** is one of three pigs that take over the education of the barnyard animals when Old Major dies. He is representative of Stalin in his willingness to desecrate and in his corruption, though he also shares characteristics with the French leader who at one point in history seemed heroic for overthrowing French royalty. Napoleon, however, makes no contributions to the farm, through policy or through work. The only thing he does is train a litter of puppies to work as his army; they eventually chase Snowball away from the farm. He represents extreme political tyranny.

Snowball is "a more vivacious pig than Napoleon, quicker in speech and more inventive, but was not considered to have the same depth of character." Unlike Napoleon, he throws himself into his work, and schemes to spread animalism and to improve the superstructure of the farm. He is like Trotsky, for whom Orwell had respect. Though he has enough charisma, he doesn't have the sheer force necessary to defend himself against Napoleon.

"An enormous beast, nearly eighteen hands high ... [**Boxer**] was not of first-rate intelligence, but he was universally respected for his steadiness of character and tremendous powers of work." His name is a nod to the Boxer Rebellion, which signaled the beginning of Communism in China. He and the other horses are representative of the simple, working-class people of Britain.

Squealer is "a small, fat pig with very round cheeks, twinkling eyes, nimble movements, and a shrill voice ... He was a brilliant talker, and when he was arguing some difficult point he had a way of skipping from side to side and whisking his tail that was somehow very persuasive. The others said of Squealer that he could turn black into white." Squealer represents *Pravda*, the Russian newspaper of the 1930s; as the story unfolds and the barnyard grows more stratified, he serves as a link between Napoleon and the other animals.

Fatherly and well-respected by the other animals, **Old Major** is a purebred boar and a metaphor for Karl Marx. News that he is going to speak rouses the entire farm at the beginning of the story, and his rhetoric inspires a revolution, despite the fact that he dies three days after delivering the speech. The unfolding story pokes fun at the flimsy idealism of Old Major's ideas, as Napoleon and Snowball, who didn't even attend his speech, adapt his notions to suit their ultimately capitalist goals.

"A stout motherly mare approaching middle life, who had never quite got her figure back after her fourth foal," **Clover** is simple and suffering, though she is more perceptive than Boxer. The narration occasionally slips into her point-of-view—she's experienced enough to have seen the difference between what the farm once was and what it has become. At the end of the book, Clover is the one to realize that man and pig look the same.

The oldest animal on the farm, **Benjamin** the donkey is wizened and to some extent cynical of the revolutionary happenings. He insists that any possible changes will not mitigate suffering. When controversy over the windmill grips the farm, Benjamin is the only animal who doesn't take sides. "He refused to believe either that food would become more plentiful or that the windmill would save work. Windmill or no windmill, he said, life would go on as it had always gone on— that is, badly." The only time anyone at the farm sees him get excited is when the truck comes to take Boxer away.

Mr. Jones, the proprietor of Manor Farm, is symbolic of the generations of farmers that oppressed the animals—or the tsars, whom the Bolsheviks fought. His slump at the beginning of the novel is symbolic of the worldwide Great Depression of the 1930s. Jones' ouster at the beginning of the work represents Stalin's revolution.

A raven and Mr. Jones' pet, **Moses** is the only one not present for Old Major's speech at the beginning of the book. Many of the farm animals resent Moses, because he stays around yet does no work, but many believe in his tales of Sugarcandy Mountain, where all animals go after death. A metaphor for the church, Moses returns to the farm several years after his disappearance, with the same promises of a life beyond strife.

Mr. Pilkington owns a neighboring farm and represents the English ruling classes who eventually align themselves with Russia. When he meets with Napoleon at the end of the story, their interactions are a metaphor for the Teheran Conference of 1943, and within his compliments about the farm's efficiency lurks a suspicion. Indeed, as the relationship between the Soviet Union and its Allies was not solidified in 1945, trouble is brewing between Napoleon and Pilkington as the curtain falls.

Another neighboring farmer, **Mr. Frederick**, represents Germany. He engages in fraudulent trading with Animal Farm (paying for timber with fraudulent bank notes) and later destroys the windmill in a surprise attack. Jeffrey Meyers suggests that his name refers to Frederick the Great, the founder of the Prussian military state and Hitler's hero.

Mr. Whymper is a shrewd solicitor whom Napoleon commissions to represent the interests of Animal Farm in the human world. This human link creates some tension among the animals.

Summary and Analysis

The story of *Animal Farm* begins as evening falls upon Manor Farm. After the proprietor, Mr. Jones, has locked up, the animals gather in the big barn to hear the dream of Old Major, a prize Middle White boar and a respected elder. He sits on a raised platform as the animals file in—among them the two cart horses Boxer and Clover; Muriel the white goat; Mollie, the white mare; and Benjamin, the old donkey. When all have settled down to listen, save Moses—the raven and Mr. Jones' pet—Old Major reveals that he is close to dying, and then shares his life philosophy. "Let us face it," he says, "our lives are miserable, laborious, and short." He shares his theory that English animals are imprisoned by work and the inevitability of slaughter, and suggests emphatically that such imprisonment is not necessary. Man, Old Major insists, is the enemy of all animals; to remove Man from their predicament would result in the eradication of overwork. "What then must we do?" he asks the rapt-faced crowd, and then doesn't wait for their answer. "Why, work night and day, body and soul, for the overthrow of the human race! That is my message to you, comrades: Rebellion!" He offers some maxims to keep in mind during the revolution, such as "Whatever goes upon two legs is an enemy. Whatever goes upon four legs, or has wings, is a friend." When several rats crept out of their holes, provoking the dogs, Old Major prompts a vote that declares rats—and all animals—equal. He then recounts his dream, of a world where man has vanished, and remembers aloud the song his mother once sang—"Beasts of England"—about the overthrow of Man. The entire population of animals begins singing the song, louder and stronger, until Mr. Jones is awakened—the gunshot he fires scatters the animals, and all settle down for the night.

Animal Farm is a modern fable about the Russian Revolution and a morality tale about what happens when the oppressed remove their oppressor. Because Orwell has created an entirely realistic world where animal thought and rationale reigns, the book is often compared to Swift's *Gulliver's Travels*; in 1946 Orwell wrote: "The durability of *Gulliver's Travels* goes to show that, if the force of belief is behind it, a world-view which only just passes the test of sanity is sufficient to produce a great work of art." Many critics argue that *Animal Farm* is especially effective because of the barnyard creatures' humanity. No single character in *Animal Farm*—unlike Orwell's other protagonists, such as *Nineteen Eighty-Four*'s Winston Smith—represents the author's point of view. Critic Patrick Reilly says the lack of focus on a single character and the admission of animals lends the prose a decisive quality: "the choice of animals rather than human beings gave Orwell for the first time a certain latitude, release from that sense of moral constraint that otherwise held him captive...the liberating secret lay in making animals behave like men." When the class divisions between man and beast are shattered, new stratifications arise among beasts. Such a resolution shows, according to Stephen Sedley, that "in politics people are no better than animals: their traditional rules may be feckless but ungovern them and a new tyranny will fill the place of the old."

George Orwell's interest in socialism dates back to his travels in Northern England during the mid-1930s. During the Spanish Civil War, he witnessed the Stalinist regime's long reach and its war on all suspected Trotskyist outfits; he saw firsthand how principles can be used as weapons against innocents. "For quite fifteen years I have regarded that regime with plain horror," he once said. Though *Animal Farm* can be read as Orwell's allegory for all revolutions, it is most specifically a critique of the Russian Revolution, from the fall of Nicholas II to Stalin's rise, through the forced collectivization of the early 1930s and the Great Purge Trials, and all the way to Russia's struggles with Germany and its alliance with the Allies. Mr. Jones, whom the reader meets in the first chapter, represents the absolute power of the Russian tsars; Old Major's dreams and his rhetoric embody both the Marxian thesis that the world is divided into the oppressors and the oppressed and Lenin's revolutionary rhetoric.

Three nights after his stirring speech, Old Major dies and is buried at the foot of the orchard. During the next three months, the work of organizing falls upon the other pigs, since they are generally considered to be the most intelligent of the animals. Snowball, Napoleon, and Squealer work with Old Major's rhetoric until they have developed a complete thought system—Animalism. They begin holding secret, late-night meetings at which they convince the more ignorant animals—among them Mollie, the white mare—that the struggle is necessary. Many animals are initially skeptical about how they will benefit from the revolution, and they raise basic concerns: "Mr. Jones feeds us. If he were gone, we should starve to death." When Moses chimes in to the conversation, he often offers distracting tales of Sugarcandy Mountain, where lump sugar and linseed cake grow on bushes. While these meetings continue through the early spring, Mr. Jones sinks further into an economic slump. He loses money in a lawsuit and spends entire days drinking and listlessly reading the newspapers. His fields lie fallow, the animals neglected and hungry. On Midsummer's Eve, Mr. Jones travels to Willingdon and drinks so much that he doesn't return until the next morning. When he arrives, he quickly falls asleep on the couch—forgetting, once more, to feed the animals. In a fit of frustration one of the cows kicks open the feed storehouse door, which prompts Mr. Jones and his four men to whip all the hungry, searching animals that enter. Suddenly and with one accord, the animals attack their masters, and, shocked, the men flee. Upon realizing what has happened, Mrs. Jones flings a few things into a carpet bag and escapes as well. When the animals finally realize their success, they search the farm grounds for any trace of human beings, remove and discard all artifacts of their imprisonment—the bits, nose-rings, chains, and knives—and take a double portion of food.

The pigs represent Manor Farm's intelligentsia, and they prime the animals for revolution with the help of the easily swayed horses, Boxer and Clover. When regarding Animal Farm as an allegory for the Russian Revolution, the ousting of Mr. Jones directly parallels the abdication of Tsar Nicholas II. However, unlike the actual revolution of 1917, this revolution is a quick and victimless one. Nicholas II and his family were shot to death in Yekaterinburg on July 17, 1918, but Mr. Jones is simply chased away; the only evidence of his family comes later, when the pigs teach themselves with the children's old spelling books. Patrick Reilly argues that Orwell's decision to temper tragedy renders the animals more sympathetic and the plot more believable. When the animals rise the next morning, they realize that the farm and the adjoining house is theirs. As they gingerly walk single file through the house, they discover Mollie admiring herself in the mirror with one of Mrs. Jones' ribbons. She is rebuked and reminded again of how these ornaments are really representations of human bondage. After several hams hanging in the kitchen are taken out for burial, the animals resolve that the house should be preserved as a museum, and that no animal should live there. During a meeting, the pigs reveal that they have been teaching themselves to read. Snowball changes the front sign from "Manor Farm" to "Animal Farm," and when they return to the barn, they explain that Animalism can be summarized in Seven Commandments, including "Whatever goes upon two legs is an enemy," and "No animal shall sleep in a bed." Since the cows haven't been milked in 24 hours, their udders are about to burst. The pigs teach themselves how to milk the cows with their trotters, and when the other animals express interest in sharing the milk, the pigs advise them to focus on the harvest. With the animals' toil and sweat—and the pigs' supervision— they complete the harvest more quickly than Jones, and the summer continues in this productive manner. Boxer bears the brunt of the work—he asks to be awakened a half hour before the others, and adopts "I will work harder!" as his personal motto. Some of the other animals, however, don't have such favorable reactions to the new regime. Mollie shirks her responsibilities, often leaving work early because of a stone in her foot, and Benjamin, the oldest member of the farm, seems cynical about the success of the Rebellion. The animals decide not to work on Sundays, reserving the day for ritual and commemorative ceremony. Every Sunday the flag is raised, the week is planned out, and resolutions are offered.

Kingsley Martin draws a parallel between Benjamin's character and Orwell's own cynicism and disillusionment—indeed, the donkey is certain that the more things change, the more they stay the same. His low, foreboding voice echoes in stark contrast to the unquestioning work of the horses. In an essay, Orwell writes that he got the idea to write *Animal Farm* after seeing a young boy whipping a cart-horse in an attempt to control it. "It struck me that if only such animals became aware of their strength we should have no power over them," Orwell writes, "and that men exploit animals in much the same way as the rich exploit the proletariat." Now that the initial rebellion has passed, however, and Animal Farm's base of power is consolidated into the hands of a few pigs, these commemoration ceremonies are used to reinforce the animals' loyalty to the cause. The hoof-and-horn flag over Animal Farm is quite similar to the Russian hammer and sickle flag, symbolic of the Red Army.

Raiding Mr. Jones' abandoned library, the pigs study blacksmithing, carpentry, and other industrial arts. Snowball organizes committees to ensure productivity. Biographer Michael Shelden writes: "As his name suggests, it is not enough for Snowball to let revolution develop according to its own momentum. He must speed it along and increase its efficiency by organizing Animal Committees, such as the Clean Tails League for the cows and the Wild Comrades Re-education Committee, the object of which is to tame rats and rabbits." Reading and writing classes help most of the more ignorant animals, though some of them are unable to learn even the Seven Commandments. Snowball insists that all seven can be summed up as "four legs good, two legs bad," and when the birds complain, he rationalizes that wings should be regarded as legs for their propulsion function. This adaptation of the truth is another example of the twisting of Marxist rhetoric in order to justify a certain action. In the meantime, Napoleon, who claims educating the young as a priority, takes a new litter of puppies and trains them. The supply of extra milk from the cows and the early windfall of apples are set aside for the pigs, and though some of the animals protest—thinking that this surplus ought to be shared equally—Squealer rationalizes that the pigs, as brainworkers, needed the extra fortification in order to keep Mr. Jones from returning: "'Milk and apples (it has been proved by Science, comrades) contain substances absolutely necessary for the well-being of a pig.... It is for your sake that we drink that milk and eat those apples.'"

According to biographer Bernard Crick, Orwell gave a copy of *Animal Farm* to his friend Geoffrey Gorer, having marked this section with a note that this "was the key passage." Indeed, this scene marks the moment when the pigs first assert power for themselves, and the animals didn't take the personal accountability to protest on their own behalf. "The problem examined by *Animal Farm* concerns the nature of revolution itself," writes V.C. Letemendia. "Unless everyone makes the revolution for him or herself without surrendering power to an elite, there will be little hope for freedom and equality." A new class stratification has arisen, which pits brainworkers against the rest of the animals. Though the pigs have been laying the foundation for this for some time, the animals' acceptance of the pigs' rationale for consumption is an example of the proletariat's weakness.

News about Animal Farm spreads as pigeons teach the "Beasts of England" dirge to farm animals across the countryside. Mr. Jones seeks solace at the Red Lion, but the farmers with whom he commiserates are more focused on using his troubles to their own advantage. Both Mr. Pilkington and Mr. Frederick, owners of the neighboring farms, assure themselves that, left to their own devices, the animals are certain to starve. When Animal Farm seems to prosper, however, the neighbors begin to spread rumors about horrible goings-on within the confines of Animal Farm, including cannibalism and torture with red-hot horseshoes. Despite the rumors, a revolutionary fever begins to grip the animals who populate the neighboring farms: "Bulls which had always been tractable suddenly turned savage, sheep broke down hedges and devoured the clover, cows kicked the pail over, hunters refused their fences and shot their riders on the other side. Above all, the tune and even the words of Beasts of England were known everywhere." In early October, Jones and a group of men enter the farm carrying sticks and guns. Snowball, who has been studying the tactics of Julius Caesar, starts the first attack against them, and a series of ambushes from the cowshed follows. In five minutes, those who have not been struck down, retreat, and Boxer later expresses remorse for the murder of a stable boy. Though Snowball insists that there's no room for sentimentality in war—"The only good human being is a dead one"—Boxer's reply is, "I have no wish to take life, not even a human life." The animals gather in the barn, give a hero's burial to a sheep—the only casualty in the struggle—and confer the honor of "Animal Hero, First Class" upon Snowball and Boxer. Jones' gun is placed at the foot of the flagstaff, and it is determined that the gun will be fired on October 12, the anniversary of the Battle of the Cowshed.

Though the notion of violence is ever apparent in *Animal Farm*, seldom is it rendered graphically. There is a method to this suppression, according to Reilly: "Existence becomes endurable as an aesthetic phenomenon," he says. The purpose of Orwell's fable, in other words, is not to diminish the horror of the Stalinist regime or the host of other dictators, but to distance oneself from it in order to enable exploration. "To criticize Orwell for allegedly demeaning the common people by depicting them as moronically credulous brutes is to misread the book," Reilly writes. "The animal fable is devised not to insult the ordinary man but to distance Orwell from the terror..." The spread of information across the countryside is an example of the domino theory, which predicted the fall of other noncommunist states because of proximity to Communism. While U.S. presidents such as Kennedy and Johnson established a military presence in countries such as Vietnam, Pilkington and Frederick begin spreading rumors about Animal Farm. One day Mollie, who is seen talking to one of Mr. Pilkington's men, disappears. After she is discovered weeks later on the other side of the fence, wearing a scarlet ribbon around her forelock, she is never mentioned again. This is, Reilly says, another example of Orwell's downplaying the facts of history so that they fit into the barnyard framework:

"What Marxist and social philosopher Herbert Marcuse deplores as the seduction of large sections the Western working class, bribed by the tidbits of consumerism, is here depicted in terms of a fallen woman of Victorian melodrama." During the bitter winter, Snowball lays plans for farm improvements, while Napoleon insists that these plans are faulty. The farm is split into factions when Napoleon urinates on Snowball's painstakingly developed windmill plans. Only Benjamin refuses to take sides in the matter, insisting, "Windmill or no windmill, life would go on as it always had gone on—that is, badly." During a meeting about the windmill, Napoleon objects briefly, sits back down, and then rises once more. He utters a high-pitched noise that summons nine enormous dogs to chase Snowball away. Napoleon, rising to assume Old Major's position, declares the Sunday meetings and debates a waste of time. Squealer assures the animals of the nobility of Napoleon's new responsibility, using the inarguable threat of Jones as a reason to eliminate the debates. After thinking over the prospect, the animals comply, and Boxer adds "Napoleon is always right" to his motto of "I will work harder."

This scene allegorizes Stalin's rise to power and the initial abandonment of the original principles of the Russian Revolution. The corresponding real-life event is Trotsky's expulsion in 1936, and his subsequent assassination. But the elimination of Snowball's dissenting voice also ushers in a new age of fear and suffering. Three weeks after Snowball's ouster, Napoleon announces that the windmill—symbolic of Lenin's dreams of electrification and modernization—will be built after all; he insists, in fact, that the windmill was his own creation. Napoleon's plans result in a year of daily backbreaking labor for the animals. They are no longer able to rest, even on Sunday afternoons. The sheep, the horses, and even the donkeys carry stones, and Boxer bears the brunt of the load, exerting himself as much as three horses. At a Sunday assembly, Napoleon announces that trade will commence with the neighboring farms. This upsets those animals who remember, under the initial tenets of Animalism, the prohibition of animals and commerce. Squealer assures the animals that such a prohibition never existed—that it was the creation of Snowball. Likewise, when the pigs move into the farmhouse, Squealer insists that living away from the sty is appropriate to the dignity of the Leader (as he's come to call Napoleon). Clover, who thought the fourth commandment had prohibited animals' sleeping in beds, was assured by Muriel that the commandment read "No animal shall sleep in a bed *with sheets.*" These subtly perplexing changes mark the beginning of Animalism's bastardization.

During a storm in November, the animals wake in the middle of the night to find their windmill has been destroyed. Standing before the bereft crowd, Napoleon insists that Snowball is behind the evil act and issues a death sentence. According to Michael Peters, Napoleon's actions here were a last-minute decision on Orwell's part: "From Paris…Orwell checked the proofs, making one last change. When the Windmill is attacked Napoleon stays standing, instead of dropping to the ground, in a tribute to Stalin's courage in remaining in Moscow during Hitler's advance." The animals promptly resume construction on the farm, despite the cold weather and the human rumor that the windmill was destroyed because the walls were too thin. The food shortage grows only more profound in January, and this news reaches the humans as well. Napoleon disguises the storehouse shelves so that they look bountiful, and leads Mr. Whymper through the storehouse so that he'll send back a message of prosperity to the humans. During the winter of 1932–33, the Soviets also began to starve as the first Five Year Plan failed. Grain exports increased to help industrialization, but the peasants were forced to cut back further and further, almost starving in the process. Mr. Whymper's tours represent those of collective farms given to select individuals, such as George Bernard Shaw and Lady Astor, to tout the industriousness of the nation.

As food and supplies dwindle further, the hens are told that they'll need to surrender their eggs for the good of the farm. In protest, they fly up to the rafters; when they lay their eggs, the eggs fall to the floor and break. Napoleon punishes them by halting their rations; nine hens starve to death, and the remaining flock capitulates. Napoleon announces that a pile of timber shall be sold to either Mr. Pilkington or Mr. Frederick, and Snowball is seen haunting the farm by night. After this revelation, Snowball receives the blame for any bit of strife on the farm. Later, Napoleon delivers the shocking piece of news that Snowball was affiliated with Mr. Jones from the beginning. Such information puzzles Boxer, but when he raises his voice in concern, Squealer retorts with a story of Napoleon's bravery during the Battle of the Cowshed.

The hens' rebellion is a direct correlative to the suppression of kulaks in the Ukraine, and, in a larger sense, symbolic of the purges in which 20 million Soviet citizens lost their lives. Under extreme duress, peasants hid their grain and refused to give up their cattle. Once again, Reilly points out that like other tragedies in the animal fable, the scope is vastly diminished: "The allegations of industrial sabotage which issued in the Moscow showcase trials dwindle into a broken window and a blocked drain, while treason to the Revolution finds its appropriate image in a sheep urinating in a drinking-pool." One day Napoleon orders the animals to assemble in the yard, and his dogs drag forward four pigs who are accused of affiliation with Snowball—the same four who protested the abolition of the Sunday meetings. When threatened, the pigs confess that Snowball has privately admitted to his work with Mr. Jones, and when they are finished, "the dogs promptly tore their throats out." Next, the three hens who led the egg-laying rebellion confess that Snowball came to them in a dream; the confessions and executions spill forward until a pile of corpses lies at Napoleon's feet. This is one of a few occasions in *Animal Farm* in which Orwell darkens the mood to frightening: "the air was heavy with the smell of blood," he writes, "which had been unknown there since the expulsion of Jones." The surviving animals creep away together, confused by what they have just seen. Boxer reassures himself that the key to understanding is to work harder. The view of the peaceful spring evening spreads out before them, and Clover looks out at the beautiful hillside, her eyes filled with tears. "If she herself had any picture of the future, it had been of a society of animals set free from hunger and the whip, all equal, each working according to his capacity, the strong protecting the weak, as she had protected the lost brood of ducklings with her foreleg on the night of Major's speech." She begins to sing "Beasts of England," rousing the other animals, who join in until Squealer enters with news that "Beasts of England" is to be abolished.

When certain members of the group remember the Sixth Commandment, "No animal shall kill any other animal," they are reassured that the Commandment requires that no animal should be killed "*without cause.*" Napoleon begins making fewer and fewer public appearances, and when he does walk around the farm, he does so with his army of dogs surrounding him. Construction on the windmill continues as the pigs compose poems to Napoleon and invent titles for him such as "Terror of Mankind." Napoleon informs the animals that Frederick has bought the pile of timber—when, a few days later, it is revealed that the bank notes are forgeries, Napoleon proclaims, "Death to Frederick!" This fiasco represents the short-lived Russo-German alliance of 1939, according to Robert A. Lee. The next day Frederick and some of his men come through the gate and blow up the windmill, inciting the animals, who—in a violent struggle that resulted in several casualties and the splitting of Boxer's hoof—chased them down the field. Squealer proclaims victory to a confused crowd of animals. Days later a strange celebration is heard from inside the farmhouse; the next morning a dull-eyed Squealer suggests that Napoleon is dying. In fact, he is hung over, and soon the pigs lay plans for brewing and even sowing barley.

Clover and Benjamin urge Boxer to retire, but he refuses, saying that his only remaining dream is to see the construction of the windmill. As winter looms again, rations are cut back for all animals but dogs and pigs—and there are 31 new pigs and plans for a schoolroom. Soon every pig receives a ration of barley and wears a green ribbon on his tail on Sundays. Napoleon orders the institution of the Spontaneous Demonstration, in which the animals will suddenly abandon their work and march around the farm, celebrating the triumphs and struggles of Animal Farm. Moses returns with news of Sugarcandy Mountain, and the pigs allow him to stay.

Reilly, examining Moses' return in Marxian terms, argues that Moses's continued prophesying on a supposedly liberated farm marks a failure for Animalism. Boxer returns to work with the approach of his twelfth birthday, and one day in the summer, he falls—complaining of his lung and resigning himself to retirement—and wonders aloud if he might be permitted to retire along with Benjamin. After awhile Squealer emerges with the news that Boxer is to be treated at a hospital in Willingdon, assuring the animals that his case will be better treated there. As he's taken away, Benjamin screams that on the side of the van was written "Alfred Simmonds, Horse Slaughterer and Glue Boiler," and Clover urges Boxer to try to escape. Still, he is wheeled away, and a few days later Squealer tells the animals that Boxer has died peacefully—his dying words, "Long live Comrade Napoleon!"—and insists that the van that took him away was purchased from the knacker. Benjamin represents the modern intellectual, says Richard I. Smyer: "Unlike his mental inferiors, he is cursed with the dispiriting awareness of the inevitable degeneration of revolutionary idealism." The day of the banquet, a grocer from Willingdon deliveres a large wooden crate to the farmhouse, and soon word goes around that the pigs have acquired another large case of whisky.

Years pass, and soon no one remembers the Rebellion except Clover, Moses, Benjamin, and the pigs. The finished windmill is used for milling corn, and Napoleon, who has grown heavy, insists that the truest happiness lies in living frugally. One day Squealer commands a crowd of sheep to follow him into a field, and they are taught a new song. One day, after the sheep have returned, Clover neighes violently at the sight of Squealer walking on his hind legs. The sheep began bleating "Four legs good, two legs *better*." Benjamin and Clover, dejected, walk over to the side of the barn—the site of the Seven Commandments—and Clover asks Benjamin to read what is written: "All Animals are Equal, but Some Animals are More Equal than Others." This haunting revision echoes through the remaining pages of the book. Raymond Williams says that he is not surprised that this statement has been used, universally, as a satire on revolution, as it successfully covers the gap between pretense and reality.

No animal is shocked when they see the pigs carrying whips in their trotters. One evening, a group of neighboring farmers are invited to the farm, and Clover and some of the other animals push into the farmhouse, curious to see a dozen farmers and half a dozen pigs gathered around the table. Mr. Pilkington toasts to the prosperity of Animal Farm, and Napoleon rises to his feet and reports on several recent changes, including the removal of the hoof and horn from the green flag and the revival of the name "The Manor Farm." "If you have your lower animals to contend with," Mr. Pilkington says, "we have our lower classes!" Clover's eyes dart between pig and man as she realizes that she cannot distinguish one from the other.

Though at one point Napoleon espoused the rhetoric of Old Major and appeared to fight for animal equality, he now sides with the humans and laughs over the folly of the lesser animals. Indeed, the revolution has come full circle, with the pigs firmly entrenched in the role of the oppressor. Likewise, the style at the end of the book is elegiac. It is, Reilly writes, "the same melancholic chord that sounds through Matthew Arnold's famous poem 'Dover Beach,' bringing 'the eternal note of sadness in.'" Punctuating the elegy, however, are the cold facts. "It was a pig walking on his hind legs," Orwell writes. "He carried a whip in his trotter." The distillation of the new farm order is impossibly simple, as well, and Orwell's vision of the Russian hypocrisy: "All animals are equal, but some animals are more equal than others." Kingsley Martin compliments this passage as being the best part of the story: "We've all noticed, with a wry smile, the gradual change of the Soviet doctrine under the pretense that it is no change and then that the original doctrine was an anti-Marxist error." The pigs' meeting with the farmers is a symbol of the Teheran Conference, when Stalin met with Winston Churchill and Franklin D. Roosevelt. V.C. Letemendia writes that Orwell's conclusion is not necessarily a pessimistic one: "Orwell is not implying by this the hopelessness of a proletarian revolution: he rather points to the need for education and self-confidence in any working class movement if it is to remain democratic in character." Letemendia goes on to say that the text does hint at disaster for the pigs, for their attempt to mimic humanity can only be futile. The reader has only the text and his or her own ideas about revolution to determine the fate of Napoleon's regime.

Critical Views

To read, or re-read, everything Orwell wrote about Communism is to make some surprising discoveries. By Communism I mean what Orwell meant by that word: the Moscow rule-book. And I suppose it would be generally agreed that he did more to bring home to a wide public the essential nature of the Communist fraud than any Western writer, including Koestler. He was one of the first to illuminate the brutality and perfidy of Communist methods and to expose Stalin's betrayal of revolutionary idealism in the interests of the Soviet Union. In 1938, without seeking to hedge in any way, he condemned by ridicule the notorious treason trials, which, by the sheer size and effrontery of the lies embodied in them, had undermined the scepticism of many who were by no means sold on Stalin, persuading them that there must be substance of some kind behind the 'confessions' and those monstrous and lunatic accusations which Vyshinsky threw about with the air of a man dispensing platitudes. He gave his name to the concept of a nightmare society more closely approached in the Soviet Union than anywhere else in the world. He produced memorable words and phrases fixing indelibly the nastiness of Communist practices and institutions. He did all this, as a would-be Socialist, in the teeth of outraged opposition from the main body of fellow left-wing intellectuals then trying desperately to knock together some sort of a shelter for themselves with rotten planks and broken timbers salvaged from the wreck of the great Soviet experiment—and he accepted no help from the Right, which he abhorred even while he valued certain human qualities found more often on the Right than on the Left.

It was an extraordinary achievement, and the first surprise, looking back, is the economy of the means employed to pull it off. What Orwell had to say directly about the matter added lip to no more than a very small fraction of his output; certain parts of *Homage to Catalonia*; a few book reviews, a couple of dozen articles in small-circulation periodicals, a short and lambent allegory, his masterpiece, *Animal Farm*. Indeed, as far as the general public was concerned, it was *Animal Farm* that did the trick: until it appeared in 1945 Orwell was known only to the few.

(...)

In his writings on a broader scale about the nature of totalitarianism and the meaning of liberty, about the British Empire, the British social system and domestic politics, he was still fighting towards the light, still seeking to achieve those elusive certainties he had pursued for so long and now seemed farther away than ever as the shared ordeal of a nation in peril made it harder for him to maintain his highly personal rigidities. In his later war-time writings he showed quite frequently a realization that, at least as far as England was concerned, he had attributed too much that he detested to deliberate, calculated predation and too little to the more or less greedy, more or less generous, more or less kindly, more or less unimaginative, more or less lazy, more or less frightened, almost wholly muddled behaviour of the ordinary human being, rich or poor—though, of course, the rich had the harder task, quite properly, in getting past his fierce-eyed guardianship of the needle's eye. 'I do not believe', he had once written, 'that a man with £5000 a year and a man with 15/– a week either can, or will cooperate.' (This was *à propos* of Borkenau's alternative to Fascism or Communism: 'orderly reconstruction through the cooperation of all classes'.) 'The nature of their relationship is, quite simply, that the one is robbing the other, and there is no reason to think that the robber will turn over a new leaf.' The very rich, then, some of them, rob the very poor ... The less rich? The slightly less poor? Towards the end of the war Orwell was beginning to see wickedness in terms of individuals as distinct from classes.

It is against this background that the miracle of *Animal*

Farm is best considered. In a surpassingly silly book called *The Making of George Orwell* Mr Keith Aldritt avers that *Animal Farm* has been greatly overrated, the whole concept being 'only a clever form for expressing a set of opinions that have been held so long that they no longer admit the complexity of the experience they claim to explain'. Leaving aside the fact that in *Animal Farm* there is no claim to explain anything at all, the central fact about it is that it is the only book which shows what Orwell could do when he had made up his mind about a subject all the way through. What Mr Aldritt calls 'Orwell's long-nurtured cynicism about Communism' (an unhappy phrase to characterize the blazing anger, contempt and pity of a man made vulnerable by his lack of even the thinnest shield of cynicism) was the outcome of an immediate, direct and passionate rejection of a combination of disgusting qualities in which he could find no redeeming feature. When he is writing about the poor and oppressed, about the mental contortions of the Left, about the selfishness of the rich, about many other things, his attack, while shattering in detail and deeply penetrating, is, in the long run, uncertain—blunted here, exaggerated there— precisely because he was always at the back of his mind aware of features which could and did redeem. This man who was for ever insisting on arrangements in sharp black and white, had great trouble in reaching a firm and settled attitude towards a complex problem. About a few things he knew just where he stood: about, for example, hanging, about colonial rule. And it was because of this, and his consequent ability to distance himself from the subject, that his two essays, 'Shooting an Elephant' and 'A Hanging' are so nearly perfect. He was also sure about Communism, as I have tried to show. For eight years he had struggled, as occasion arose, to shame and ridicule others into sharing his view. It had not been enough. In *Animal Farm* he made a supreme effort, echoing Conrad: 'It is, before all, to make you *see*.' He succeeded at last and there was no more to be done.

The astonishing thing is that this writer, whose especial value had lain in an unending, brooding, irritable dialogue with himself, a questioning, a doubting and a self-doubting, should have found himself able to take up a subject which was crystal clear in his mind and transmute it into a finished, wholly self-sufficient work of art, standing back and sublimating his indignation through an exercise in compassion which showed what he might have done had he been given health and time to discover his true position in face of other problems, subtler and more complex, which crowded in on him.

Matthew Hodgart on *Animal Farm* as Satire, Fable, and Allegory

The starting-point of any successful satire is a militant, combative attitude to political experience, and in particular to the politics of the satirists' own peers, the writers and intellectuals, who ought to know better. This was the starting-point of the greatest of English satirists, as Orwell pointed out in another memorable essay ('Politics vs. Literature: an Examination of Gulliver's Travels'). He characterized Swift politically as 'one of those people who are driven into a sort of perverse Toryism by the follies of the progressive party of the moment'. To his credit, Orwell did not pervert to Toryism: he remained with the Left of the Labour Party, but his sympathy with Swift is obviously very deep, despite some unfair and even unscholarly comments on Swift's politics. When I read this essay in 1946, I wrote to Orwell to the effect that he had not mentioned the affair of the Drapier's Letters, when Swift personally took on the English Ascendancy in Ireland, at great personal risk (though not a traitor could be found, to sell him for six hundred pound); and for this and other reasons Swift deserved the description of himself in his epitaph as 'strenuous champion of liberty'. Orwell replied politely, but on this point, I thought, evasively: I am sure that if he had thought more about Swift and Ireland he would have been able to justify more adequately the admiration he shows for Swift as a writer. In fact, the intense pessimism of *Nineteen Eighty-Four*, the pity expressed for the proles and contempt poured on the educated, the emphasis on physical disgust and finally on madness, place Orwell very close to Swift.

The second prerequisite of successful satire is the right medium. Satire has to be funny or it remains mere polemic and satiric humour demands travesty, the vision of the world upside-down. The number of ways in which travesty can be presented is evidently limited, and classic satire has usually been confined to a rather small number of traditional *genres*: the traveller's tale; the moral fable, and so on. The satiric *genres* are often travesties of the serious *genres* of literature, and parody is the main technique by which the one is transformed into the other, as epic into mock-heroic. The writer's main pleasure and *élan* will come from the ingenuity demanded by parody and the aggressive mockery that it releases. There is probably a fair amount of luck in the creation of satire. Even if the satirist has found the right subject and worked up a properly belly-feeling approach to it, he still has to find the form: he may never do so, but if he does the satire will practically write itself. This must have been the case with *Animal Farm*, a gay, fluent work, completed in a few months in the midst of Orwell's wartime preoccupations. He chose a very ancient *genre*, based on the animal story found in the folk-tales of all primitive and peasant cultures, and reflecting a familiarity and sympathy with animals which Orwell seems to have shared. The central figure is often the trickster, spider in Africa, fox in Europe and pig in Orwell. The Aesopian fable, perfected by La Fontaine, is a sophisticated version, which carries a moral or political lesson; still more elaborate are the medieval beast-epics of Renart, represented in English by Chaucer's tale of Chaunticlere. Orwell tells us that the idea came to him from the sight of an animal, a huge cart-horse driven by a little boy, who was whipping it whenever it tried to turn. 'It struck me that if only such animals became aware of their strength we should have no power over them, and that men exploit animals in much the same way as the, rich exploit the proletariat.' Thus Boxer, representing the long-suffering Russian workers and peasants, is the hero of the tale. Once he had this image in his head, Orwell went on to develop Old

Major's (Marx's) theory of revolution as applied to animals. He used the animal-story tradition with great confidence and deftness, and since he wanted to reach the widest possible world public, through translation, he also parodied the style of children's books; but not patronizingly, since Orwell, I think, liked children as much as he liked animals. Although the betrayal of the revolution is a 'sad story' it is told with the straightness that children demand, and with childlike cunning and charm.

Animal Farm also belongs to the *genre* of allegory, since it has a point-to-point correspondence with the events of Russian history from 1917 to 1943: the war of intervention, the New Economic Plan, the First Five-year Plan, the expulsion of Trotsky and the seizing of supreme power by Stalin, the Stakhanovites, the Hitler–Stalin Pact and the invasion by Germany are all clearly figured.* It is also an apocalypse, like the Book of Daniel or the sixth book of the *Aeneid*, in that it moves imperceptibly from the past through the present (of which the account though fictionalized is basically true) to the future. It therefore ends with prophecy. Though literally the last episode, when the pigs sit down to drink with the farmers, is meant to represent the Teheran Conference, when Stalin met the Allied leaders, it is also a forecast of Russian politics. And to some extent it has come true, in that the Russians have become just as imperialistic, in their handling of subject peoples, as any of the empires of the past.

Note
*See Howard Fink, *Animal Farm Notes*, Coles, Toronto, 1965.

RAYMOND WILLIAMS ON THE STRUGGLE BETWEEN ANIMALS AND HUMANS

Past the easy exploitation and the equally easy rejection, the fable in *Animal Farm* offers positive and negative evidence of a permanently interesting kind.

Orwell got the germ of the fable from seeing

> a little boy, perhaps ten years old, driving a huge cart-horse along a narrow path, whipping it whenever it tried to turn. It struck me that if only such animals became aware of their strength we should have no power over them, and that men exploit animals in much the same way as the rich exploit the proletariat.[3]

This insight is already of a rather different kind from the eventual projection. The speed of his figurative transition from animals to the proletariat is interesting, showing as it does a residue of thinking of the poor as animals, powerful but stupid. Men, of course, here and in the story, are seen as exploiters. And the worst thing about the Bolshevik pigs, in the story, is that they become indistinguishable from drunken, greedy, and cruel men. The noble beast is the workhorse Boxer.

It is worth considering this alongside Orwell's remarks on Swift's Houyhnhnms and Yahoos.[4] He is quick to diagnose Swift's disgust with man and apparent preference for animals, but he goes on to say that actually the Houyhnhnms, whom he finds unattractive, are more like men than the Yahoos, who are a deliberate degradation. Very complicated feelings are involved here. The powerful but stupid horses of *Animal Farm* are looked on with great respect and pity. The men and the pigs are intelligent, calculating, greedy, and cruel. This is surely more than a simple operative analogy. It is a substantial, even physical, response.

The other element of the analogy is exploitation. If *they* became aware of their strength, *we* should have no power over them. Orwell here is thinking about something more than a political event, about a range of relations in man's use of animals and of nature. The point he goes on to is in any other terms very surprising:

> I proceeded to analyse Marx's theory from the animals' point of view. To them it was clear that the concept of a class struggle between humans was pure illusion, since whenever it was necessary to exploit animals, all humans

united against them: the true struggle is between animals and humans. From this point of departure, it was not difficult to elaborate the story.[5]

The true struggle between animals and humans: is that the real theme of *Animal Farm*? It is difficult to say so, without most of the surface of the story collapsing. What really happens, I think, is that the very deep identification between the laboring and exploited animals and the laboring and exploited poor is retained, almost unnoticed, as a base for the exposure of that "pure illusion ... of a class struggle between humans"—humans, now, being capitalists and revolutionaries, the old ruling class and the new, who, whatever their differences and their conflicts, can be depended upon to go on exploiting the creatures on whose backs they live, and even, as at the end of the story, to unite against them. Orwell is opposing here more than the Soviet or Stalinist experience. Both the consciousness of the workers and the possibility of authentic revolution are denied.

These denials, I would say, are inhuman. But it is part of the paradox of Orwell that from this despairing base he is able to generate an immediate and practical humanity: the comradeship of the suffering, which he feels very deeply, and also, more actively, the critical skepticism of the exploited, an unexpected kind of consciousness that informs the story. I have said that *Animal Farm* is unique among Orwell's books because it contains no Orwell figure, no isolated man who breaks from conformity but is then defeated and reabsorbed. This figure is, rather, projected into a collective action: this is what happens to the animals who free themselves and then, through violence and fraud, are again enslaved.

The collective projection has a further effect. What happens is a common rather than an isolated experience, for all its bitterness; and the whine of ragged nerves, the despair of a lonely trajectory are replaced by an actively communicative tone in the critical narrative. A paradoxical confidence, an assured and active and laughing intelligence, is manifested in the very penetration and exposure of the experience of defeat. Through this mode, Orwell is able to release an exceptionally strong and pure prose. "All animals are equal ... but some are more equal than others." It is not surprising that this phrase has passed into ordinary language with a meaning much stronger than that of simple satire on revolutionary betrayal. It is one of those permanent statements about the gap between pretense and actuality, profession and practice, that covers a very wide range. In many places throughout *Animal Farm*, this strong and liberating intelligence transforms a bitter perception into an active and stimulating critique. Beyond the details of the local analogy, and paradoxically beyond the more fundamental despair, this lively awareness connects and informs. Even the last sad scene, where the excluded animals look from man to pig and pig to man and cannot tell which is which, carries a feeling that is more than disillusion and defeat. Seeing that they are the same because they act the same, never mind the labels and the formalities—that is a moment of gained consciousness, a potentially liberating discovery. In its small scale and within its limited terms, *Animal Farm* has a radical energy that goes far beyond its occasion and has its own kind of permanence.

Notes
3. *Collected Essays,* ... III, 406.
4. *Ibid.,* IV, 217–19.
5. *Ibid.,* III, 406.

GRAHAM GREENE ON LITERARY RESPONSIBILITY DURING WARTIME

Whatever you may say about writers—their private lives, their feeding habits or their taste in shirts—you have to admit, I think, that there has never been such a thing as a literature of appeasement.

Writers may pass, like everyone else, through the opium dream of Munich and Yalta, but no literature comes out of that dream.

For literature is concerned above everything else with the accurate expression of a personal vision, while appeasement is a matter of compromise.

Nevertheless, in wartime there has to be a measure of appeasement, and it is as well for the writer to keep quiet. He must not give way to despondency or dismay, he must not offend a valuable ally, he must not even make fun ...

It is a welcome sign of peace that Mr George Orwell is able to publish his 'fairy story' *Animal Farm*, a satire upon the totalitarian state and one state in particular. I have heard a rumour that the manuscript was at one time submitted to the Ministry of information, that huge cenotaph of appeasement, and an official there took a poor view of it. 'Couldn't you make them some other animal,' he is reported as saying in reference to the dictator and his colleagues, 'and not pigs?'

For this is the story of a political experiment on a farm where the animals, under the advice of a patriarchal porker, get organised and eventually drive out Mr Jones, the human owner.

The porker does not live to see the success of his revolution, but two other pigs, Snowball and Napoleon, soon impose their leadership on the farm animals. Never had the farm animals worked with such élan for Mr Jones as they now work, so they believe, for themselves. They have a song, 'Beasts of England'; they have the inspiring seven commandments of Animalism, taught them by the old porker, painted on the barn for all to see.

1. Whoever goes upon two legs is an enemy.
2. Whatever goes upon four legs, or has wings, is a friend.
3. No animal shall wear clothes.
4. No animal shall sleep in a bed.
5. No animal shall drink alcohol.
6. No animal shall kill any other animal.
7. All animals are equal.

They have a banner which blows over the farmhouse garden, a hoof and horn in white painted on an old green tablecloth.

It is a sad fable, and it is an indication of Mr Orwell's fine talent that it is really sad—not a mere echo of human failings at one remove. We do become involved in the fate of Molly the Cow, old Benjamin the Donkey, and Boxer the poor devil of a hard-working, easily deceived Horse. Snowball is driven out by Napoleon, who imposes his solitary leadership with the help of a gang of savage dogs, and slowly the Seven Commandments become altered or erased, until at last on the barn door appears only one sentence. 'All animals are equal, but some animals are more equal than others.'

If Mr Walt Disney is looking for a real subject, here it is: it has all the necessary humour, and it has, too, the subdued lyrical quality he can sometimes express so well. But is it perhaps a little too real for him? There is no appeasement here.

KINGSLEY MARTIN ON ORWELL'S CYNICISM AND BENJAMIN

Mr Orwell's Devils have been numerous and, since he is a man of integrity, he chooses real evils to attack. His latest satire, beautifully written, amusing and, if you don't take it too seriously, a fair corrective of much silly worship of the Soviet Union, suggests to me that he is reaching the exhaustion of idealism and approaching the bathos of cynicism. He began as a civil servant, honestly indignant with the misdeeds of the British Empire as he saw it in the Far East. During the Spanish war, a sincere anti-Fascist, he found, like many others of his temperament, that of all the warring groups the most idealistic and least smirched were the anarchists. The fact that they would infallibly have lost the war while the Republican coalition might, in slightly more favourable circumstances, have won it, did not affect his onslaught. At the outset of the World War he repented his past. Realising that Nazi Germany was now an even worse enemy than the British Empire or the Negrin Government, he wrote denouncing the Left. scarcely noticing that it was his own back he was lashing, and that his blows often fell short of others who had not made the mistakes with which he charged them. Now that Germany is defeated, it seems almost accidental that his righteous indignation is turned not, say, against the Americans for their treatment of Negroes, but against the Soviet Union. In Stalin he finds the latest incarnation of Evil.

There is plenty in the U.S.S.R. to satirise, and Mr Orwell does it well. How deftly the fairy story of the animals who, in anticipation of freedom and plenty, revolt against the tyrannical farmer, turns into a rollicking caricature of the Russian Revolution! His shafts strike home. We all know of the sheep, who drown discussion by the bleating of slogans; we have all noticed, with a wry smile, the gradual change of Soviet doctrine under the pretence that it is no change and then that the original doctrine was an anti-Marxist error. (The best thing in Mr Orwell's story is the picture of the puzzled animals examining the Original Principles of the Revolution, and finding them altered: 'All animals are equal,' said the slogan; to which is added, 'but some are more equal than others.') The falsehoods about Trotsky, whose part in the revolutionary period, only secondary to Lenin's, has been gradually erased from the Soviet history books, is another fair count against Stalinite methods. The story of the loyal horse who worked until his lungs burst and was finally sent of to the knackers' yard is told with a genuine pathos; it represents a true and hateful aspect of every revolutionary struggle. Best of all is the character of the donkey who says little, but is always sure that the more things change the more they will be the same, that men will always be oppressed and exploited whether they have revolutions and high ideals or not.

The logic of Mr Orwell's satire is surely the ultimate cynicism of Ben, the donkey. That, if I read Mr Orwell's mind correctly, is where his idealism and disillusion has really landed him. But he has not quite the courage to see that he has lost faith, not in Russia but in mankind. So the surface moral of his story is that all would have gone well with the revolution if the wicked Stalin had not driven the brave and good Trotsky out of Eden. Here Mr Orwell ruins what should have been a very perfect piece of satire on human life. For by putting the Stalin–Trotsky struggle in the centre he invites every kind of historical and factual objection. We are brought from the general to the particular; to the question why Stalin decided to attempt the terrific feat of creating an independent Socialist country rather than risk plunging Russia unprepared into a war of intervention by stirring up revolution in neighbouring countries. Mr Orwell may say it would have been better if this policy had prevailed, but a moment's thought will evoke in him the brilliant satire he would have written about the betrayal of the revolution, if Trotsky, who was as ruthless a revolutionary as Stalin, had won the day and lost the revolution by another route. This same error compels the reader to ask whether in fact it is true that the Commissar today is indistinguishable in ideals and privilege from the Tzarist bureaucrat and the answer is that though many traditional Russian characteristics survive in Russia, the new ruling class is really very different indeed from anything that Russia has known before. In short, if we read the satire as a gibe at the failings of the U.S.S.R. and realise that it is historically false and neglectful of the complex truth about Russia, we shall enjoy it and be grateful for our laugh. But which will Mr Orwell do next? Having fired his bolt against Stalin, he could return to the attack on British or American Capitalism as seen through the eyes say, of an Indian peasant; the picture would be about as true or as false. Alternatively, there is the Church of Rome, Yogi, or at a pinch, the more tedious effort to help find the solution of any of the problems that actually face Stalin, Mr Attlee, Mr Orwell and the rest of us.

CYRIL CONNOLLY ON THE BETRAYAL OF THE RUSSIAN REVOLUTION

Mr Orwell is a revolutionary who is in love with 1910. This ambivalence constitutes his strength and his weakness. Never before has a progressive political thinker been so handicapped by nostalgia for the Edwardian shabby-genteel or the under-dog. It is this political sentimentality which from the literary point of view is his most valid emotion. Animal Farm proves it, for it truly is a fairy story told by a great lover of liberty and a great lover of animals. The farm is real, the animals are moving. At the same time it is a devastating attack on Stalin and his 'betrayal' of the Russian revolution, as seen by another revolutionary. The allegory between the animals and the fate of their revolution (they drive out the human beings and plan a Utopia entrusted to the leadership of the pigs—Napoleon–Stalin, Snowball–Trotsky—with the dogs as police, the sheep as yes-men, the two cart-horses, Boxer and Clover, as the noble hard-working proletariat), and the Russian experiment is beautifully worked out, perhaps the most felicitous moment being when the animal 'saboteurs' are executed for some of the very crimes of the Russian trials, such as the sheep who confessed to having 'urinated in the drinking pool' or the goose which kept back six ears of corn and ate them in the night. The fairy tale ends with the complete victory of Napoleon and the pigs, who rule Animal Farm with a worse tyranny and a far greater efficiency than its late human owner, the dissolute Mr Jones.

(...)

It is arguable that every revolution is 'betrayed' because the violence necessary to achieve it is bound to generate an admiration for violence which leads to the abuse of power. A revolution is the forcible removal of an obsolete and inefficient ruling-class by a vigorous and efficient one which replaces it for as long as its vitality will allow. The commandments of the Animal Revolution, such as 'no animal shall kill any other animal' or 'all animals are equal' can perhaps never be achieved by a revolutionary seizure of power but only by the spiritual operation of reason or moral philosophy in the animal heart. If we look at Russia without the particular bitterness of the disappointed revolutionary we see that it is an immensely powerful managerial despotism—far more powerful than its Czarist predecessor—where, on the whole, despite a police system which we should find intolerable, the masses are happy, and where great strides in material progress have been made (i.e. independence of women, equality of sexes, autonomy of racial and cultural minorities, utilization of science to improve the standard of living, religious toleration, etc.). If Stalin and his regime were not loved as well as feared the Animal Farm which comprises the greatest land-mass of the world would not have united to roll back the most efficient invading army which the world has ever known—and if in truth Stalin is loved then he and his regime cannot be quite what they appear to Mr Orwell (indeed Napoleon's final brutality to Boxer—if Boxer symbolises the proletariat, is not paralleled by any incident in Stalin's career—unless the Scorched Earth policy is indicated). But it is unfair to harp on these considerations. *Animal Farm* is one of the most enjoyable books since the war, it is deliciously written, with something of the feeling, the penetration and the verbal economy of Orwell's master, Swift.

ISAAC ROSENFELD ON THE "POINT" OF *ANIMAL FARM*

Animal Farm, a brief barnyard history of the Russian Revolution from October to just beyond the Stalin–Hitler pact, is the characteristic product of such a mind, both with credit and discredit to its qualities. It puts an imaginative surface on the facts, but does not go far beneath the surface and shows little in excess of the minimum of invention necessary to make the transposition into an animal perspective. The facts are straight, and all the wieldy ones are there; the interpretation, within these limits, is plain and true. The implicit moral attitude toward the real historical events is one of an indignation that goes-without-saying, opposed to the nonsense and chicanery of Party dialectics, and to what has come to be recognized, to a large extent through Orwell's writing, as the well-intentioned, peculiarly liberal act of submission to the tyrant's myth. At least by implication, Orwell again makes clear in this book his allegiance to an older and more honorable liberalism that still holds as its dearest thing the right to liberty of judgment. Nevertheless, this is a disappointing piece of work; its best effort is exerted somewhere on middle ground, between the chuckle-headed monstrosity of orthodox Stalinism and the sated anti-Stalinist intelligence of long standing which already knows all this and a good deal more besides.

In brief, old Major, the pig, shortly before his death, delivers himself of the lessons of his life for the benefit of the animals of Mr Jones's Manor Farm, pointing out to them how they have been exploited by Man (capitalism) and urging the revolutionary establishment of a better society (The Communist Manifesto). The animals drive Mr Jones off the farm and hold it against his attempts to regain possession (Revolution and defeat of the Counter-revolution). Led by two pigs, Napoleon (Stalin), more or less in the background, and Snowball (Trotsky, with a soupçon of Lenin—for simplicity's sake, Vladimir Ilyitch is left out of the picture, entering it only as a *dybbuk*[1] who shares with Marx old Major's identity, and with Trotsky, Snowball's) the animals institute a regime free of Man, based on collective ownership, socialized production, equality, etc. The pigs, who are the most intelligent animals, form a bureaucracy which does not at first enjoy many privileges, this development being held over until the factional dispute over the rate of industrialization and the strategy of World Revolution begins, Snowball-Trotsky is exiled, and Napoleon-Stalin comes to power. Then we have, in their animal equivalent, the important episodes of hardship and famine, growth of nationalism, suspension of workers' rights and privileges, frame-ups, Moscow Trials, fake confessions, purges, philosophical revisions—'All animals are equal' becoming, 'All animals are equal, but some animals are more equal than others'—the Stalin–Hitler pact, etc.—all of which is more interesting as an exercise in identification than as a story in its own right.

What I found most troublesome was the question that attended my reading—what is the point of *Animal Farm*? is it that the pigs, with the most piggish pig supreme, will always disinherit the sheep and the horses? If so, why bother with a debunking fable; why not, *à la* James Burnham, give assent to the alleged historical necessity? But it is not so—for which we have Orwell's own word in a recent article in *Polemic* attacking Burnham.[2] And if we are not to draw the moldy moral of the pig, what then?

Though Orwell, I am sure, would not seriously advance the bad-man theory of history, it appears that he has, nevertheless, drawn on it for the purpose of writing *Animal Farm*. There are only two motives operating in the parable (which is already an oversimplification to the point of falsity, if we take the parable as intended); one of them, a good one, Snowball's, is defeated, and the only other, the bad one, Napoleon's, succeeds, presumably because history belongs to the most unscrupulous. I do not take this to be Orwell's own position, for his work has shown that he knows it to be false and a waste of time in historical analysis; it is, however, the position of his imagination, as divorced from what he knows—a convenient ground, itself a fable, to set his fable on. (If Marxism has really failed, the most ironic thing about its failure is that it should be attributed to the piggishness of human nature.) It is at this point that a failure of imagination—failure to expand the parable, to incorporate into it something of the complexity of the real event—becomes identical with a failure in politics. The story, which is inadequate as a way into the reality, also falls short as a way out; and while no one has a right to demand of *Animal Farm* that it provide a solution to the Russian problem—something it never set out to do—it is nevertheless true that its political relevance is more apparent than real. It will offer a kind of enlightenment to those who still need it, say, the members of the Book of the Month Club, but beyond this it has no politics at all.

Notes

1. Yiddish for an evil spirit.
2. James Burnham is the author of *The Managerial Revolution* (1942), which influenced *1984*. Orwell's article is 'Second Thoughts on James Burnham,' *Polemic*, III (May 1946), pp. 13–33.

Animal Farm, by George Orwell, is a satirical animal fable about the progress—or backsliding—of the Russian Revolution. If you are told that the story deals with a group of cows, horses, pigs, sheep, and poultry which decide to expel their master and run his farm for themselves but eventually turn into something almost indistinguishable from human beings, with the pigs as a superior caste exploiting the other animals very much as the farmer did, and if you hear that Stalin figures as a pig named Napoleon and Trotsky as a pig named Snowball, you may not think it sounds particularly promising. But the truth is that it is absolutely first-rate. As a rule, I have difficulty in swallowing these modern animal fables; I can't bear Kipling's stories about the horses that resist trade-unionism and the beehive that is ruined by Socialism[1], nor have I ever been able to come under the spell of *The Wind in the Willows*. But Mr Orwell has worked out his theme with a simplicity, a wit, and a dryness that are closer to La Fontaine and Gay, and has written in a prose so plain and spare, so admirably proportioned to his purpose, that *Animal Farm* even seems very creditable if we compare it with Voltaire and Swift.

Mr Orwell, before the war, was not widely known in America or even, I think, in England. He is one of several English writers who were only just beginning to be recognized in those years of confusion and tension and whose good work was obscured and impeded while the war was going on. But I think that he is now likely to emerge as one of the ablest and most interesting writers that the English have produced in this period, and, since he is now getting a reputation in this country, I should like to recommend to publishers that they look up his early novels and memoirs. There is a novel of his called *Burmese Days*, a title deceptively suggestive of reminiscences by a retired official, which is certainly one of the few first-hand and really excellent pieces of fiction that have been written about India since Kipling. Orwell's book is not the set piece and tour de force that E. M. Forster's *A Passage to*

India was; but the author, who was born in Bengal and served in the Burmese police, is 'saturated' with his subject, where Forster had to get his up. This book (which, I understand, was allowed to appear in England only in a text that had been modified under pressure of the India Office) attracted, so far as I remember, no attention whatever when it came out over here, but it ought certainly to be republished, with a more striking and appropriate title. It is illuminating as a picture of Burma and distinguished as a work of literature.

Note
1. 'A Walking Delegate' and 'The Mother Hive.'

NORTHROP FRYE ON THE SUCCESS AND FAILURE OF *ANIMAL FARM'S* VARIOUS SATIRES

George Orwell's satire on Russian Communism, *Animal Farm*, has just appeared in America, but its fame has preceded it, and surely by now everyone has heard of the fable of the animals who revolted and set up a republic on a farm, how the pigs seized control and how, led by a dictatorial boar named Napoleon, they finally became human beings walking on two legs and carrying whips just as the old Farmer Jones had done. At each stage of this receding revolution one of the seven principles of the original rebellion becomes corrupted, so that 'no animal shall kill any other animal' has added to it the words 'without cause' when there is a great slaughter of the so-called sympathizers of an exiled pig named Snowball, and 'no animal shall sleep in a bed' takes on 'with sheets' when the pigs move into the human farmhouse and monopolize its luxuries. Eventually there is only one principle left, modified to 'all animals are equal, but some are more equal than others,' as Animal Farm, its name changed back to Manor Farm, is welcomed into the community of human farms again after its neighbors have realized that it makes its 'lower' animals work harder on less food than any other farm, so that the model worker's republic becomes a model of exploited labor.

The story is very well-written, especially the Snowball episode, which suggests that the Communist 'Trotskyite' is a conception on much the same mental plane as the Nazi 'Jew,' and the vicious irony of the end of Boxer the work horse is perhaps really great satire. On the other hand, the satire on the episode corresponding to the German invasion seems to me both silly and heartless, and the final metamorphosis of pigs into humans at the end is a fantastic disruption of the sober logic of the tale. The reason for the change in method was to conclude the story by showing the end of Communism under Stalin as a replica of its beginning under the Czar. Such an alignment is, of course, complete nonsense, and as Mr Orwell must know it to be nonsense, his motive for adopting it was presumably that he did not know how otherwise to get his allegory rounded off with a neat epigrammatic finish.

Animal Farm adopts one of the classical formulas of satire, the corruption of principle by expediency, of which Swift's *Tale of a Tub* is the greatest example. It is an account of the bogging down of Utopian aspirations in the quicksand of human nature which could have been written by a contemporary of Artemus Ward[1] about one of the co-operative communities attempted in America during the last century. But for the same reason it completely misses the point as a satire on the Russian development of Marxism, and as expressing the disillusionment which many men of goodwill feel about Russia. The reason for that disillusionment would be much better expressed as the corruption of expediency by principle. For the whole point about Marxism was surely that it was the first revolutionary movement in history which attempted to start with a concrete historical situation instead of vast a priori generalizations of the 'all men are equal' type, and which aimed at scientific rather than Utopian objectives. Marx and Engels worked out a revolutionary technique based on an analysis of history known as dialectic materialism, which appeared in the nineteenth century at a time when metaphysical materialism was a fashionable creed, but which Marx and Engels always insisted was a quite different thing from metaphysical materialism.

Today, in the Western democracies, the Marxist approach to historical and economic problems is, whether he realizes it or not, an inseparable part of the modern educated man's consciousness, no less than electrons or dinosaurs, while metaphysical materialism is as dead as the dodo, or would be if it were not for one thing. For a number of reasons, chief among them the comprehensiveness of the demands made on a revolutionary by a revolutionary philosophy, the distinction just made failed utterly to establish itself in practice as it did in theory. Official Marxism today announces on page one that dialectic materialism is to be carefully distinguished from metaphysical materialism, and then insists from page two to the end that Marxism is nevertheless a complete materialist metaphysic of experience, with materialist answers to such questions as the existence of God, the origin of knowledge and the meaning of culture. Thus instead of including itself in the body of modern thought and giving a revolutionary dynamic to that body, Marxism has become a self-contained dogmatic system, and one so exclusive in its approach to the remainder of modern thought as to appear increasingly antiquated and sectarian. Yet this metaphysical materialism has no other basis than that of its original dialectic, its program of revolutionary action. The result is an absolutizing of expediency which makes expediency a principle in itself. From this springs the reckless intellectual dishonesty which it is so hard not to find in modern Communism, and which is naturally capable of rationalizing any form of action, however ruthless.

A really searching satire on Russian Communism, then, would be more deeply concerned with the underlying reasons for its transformation from a proletarian dictatorship into a kind of parody of the Catholic Church. Mr Orwell does not bother with motivation: he makes his Napoleon inscrutably ambitious, and lets it go at that, and as far as he is concerned some old reactionary bromide like 'you can't change human nature' is as good a moral as any other for his fable. But he, like Koestler, is an example of a large number of writers in the

Western democracies who during the last fifteen years have done their level best to adopt the Russian interpretation of Marxism as their own world-outlook and have failed.

Note
1. Artemus Ward, pseudonym of Charles Browne (1834–67), an American humorist.

ROBERT PEARCE ON ORWELL AND TOLSTOY

Everyone is familiar with the parallels between Russian history and the plot of *Animal Farm*. Perhaps indeed we are over-familiar with them, for the details of the book had a wider totalitarian relevance than to any one country, and Orwell borrowed from Italian history ('Mussolini is always right') and from German, as well as from Russian. But there is one issue in the book for which there seems no real-life equivalent: this is the rewriting of the original revolutionary aims, the principles of Animalism. Admittedly revolutionary idealism in Russia and elsewhere was betrayed and perverted, but there was no outward repudiation of Marxist rhetoric. Although Stalin ignored such theory in his actions and imposed his will by force of arms and propaganda, he never ceased to pay lip-service to the original ideals. Even when he was arraigning the Old Bolsheviks in the Show Trials of the 1930s, he was at pains to assert that it was they—not he—who had sinned against the holy writ of Marxist-Leninist ideology. So what inspired Orwell's brilliant and hard-hitting reformulations?

First, we must look at the precise ways in which the Commandments of the first chapter of *Animal Farm* were perverted in the course of the book. 'No animal shall sleep in a bed' became 'No animal shall sleep in a bed *with sheets*'. 'No animal shall drink alcohol' changed into 'No animal shall drink alcohol *to excess*'. 'No animal shall kill any other animal' became 'No animal shall kill another animal *without cause*'. Most famously of all, 'All animals are equal' became 'All animals are equal but some animals are more equal than others'. In short, each commandment received a coda, a reservation which effectively reversed its meaning.

There is no parallel to this in Russian political history. But Leo Tolstoy had observed a very similar perversion, in Russian religious history, as Leon recounts in his biography. What Tolstoy considered the essential precepts of the Sermon on the Mount had become almost their opposites in the mouths of Russian Orthodox clerics. The original 'Do not be angry' had become 'Do not be angry without a *cause*'.[15] The phrase 'without a cause' was, to Tolstoy, the key to an understanding of the perversion of scripture. Of course everyone who is angry justifies himself with a cause, however trivial or unjust, and therefore he guessed, correctly as he soon found, that the words were a later interpolation designed to devalue the original injunction. Similarly the instructions not to promise anything on oath, not to resist evil by violence, and not to judge or go to law had all been overturned, and had become their opposites, when the church had sought accommodation with the civil power.

Orwell's reading of the extracts from Tolstoy in Leon's biography, as detailed above, may well have inspired his rewriting of the principles of Animalism. This, of course, is not to denigrate Orwell's achievement. It was he who had, first, to see the appositeness to his own work of the banal—but contextually brilliant—'without a cause' and, then, to invent similar reservations. But it is to insist that the provenance of the details of *Animal Farm* is far wider than the painful period of history through which Orwell lived. It is also to contend that Tolstoy was an important influence on Orwell.

Although this may be considered more speculative, it is quite possible that Orwell actually read the original Tolstoy, either before Leon's book was published or as a result of seeing its brief extracts. We do know that Orwell was prepared to search 'all over London' to track down a Tolstoyan quarry;[16] and as a bibliophile he was always well aware of new material being published, even in the dark days of 1940. The fact that, for effect, Orwell italicized his codas as did Tolstoy, though Leon's quotations were all in roman script,[17] is added evidence for this.

If he did consult the original translation by Aylmer Maude, Orwell would have found other neat reformulations by Tolstoy which may well have influenced his own. To say 'do not be angry without *a cause*', Tolstoy decided, was like urging someone to 'Love the neighbour whom thou approvest of'.[18] He also drew attention to the 1864 edition of the Catechism which, after quoting each of the Ten Commandments, then gave 'a reservation which cancelled it'. For instance, the commandment to honour one God had an addendum to the effect that we should also honour the angels and saints, 'besides, of course, the Mother of God and the three persons of the Trinity'. The second commandment, not to make idols, was perverted into an injunction to make obeisance before icons; the third, not to take oaths, became a demand to swear when called upon to do so by the legal authorities. The command to honour one's mother and father degenerated into a call to honour also the Tsar, the ministers of the church, and all those in authority—specified on three long pages! 'Thou shalt not kill' was interpreted ingeniously. One should not kill 'except in the fulfilment of one's duties'.[19]

The similarity between the methods employed in the relevant passages of Tolstoy and Orwell is astonishing. The most obvious way of accounting for this is by direct influence. There are indeed other indications that Orwell's reading and rereading of Tolstoy left its mark on his work. May not the character of Boxer in *Animal Farm* have been influenced by the long-suffering talking horse who was carried off to the knacker at the end of Tolstoy's short story 'Strider: The Story of a Horse'?

Notes

15. D. Leon, *Tolstoy: His Life and Work* (London, 1944), 200.

16. *CEJL* ii. 156.

17. Leon, *Tolstoy*, 199–200; Leo Tolstoy, *A Confession: The Gospel in Brief and What I Believe* (Oxford, 1940), 372.

18. Tolstoy, *Confession*, 373.

19. Tolstoy, *Confession*, 496–7.

Orwell's inconsistencies are reflected in his ambivalent appraisal of the work he did at the BBC and of the institution itself. In *Partisan Review* he told American readers: 'As to the accuracy of news, I believe this is the most truthful war that has been fought in modern times,'[54] And at the time he was about to join the BBC he stated: 'I believe that the BBC, in spite of the stupidity of its foreign propaganda and the unbearable voices of its announcers, is very truthful. It is generally regarded as more reliable than the press.'[55] When he left the BBC, he denied that he had any disagreement with BBC policy or that he had left on account of any kind of grievance.[56] Yet it would appear that in reporting to American readers, Orwell was still playing the role of propagandist, for in his private letters an entirely different view emerges. Informing Rayner Heppenstall about his intention of leaving the BBC, Orwell wrote:

> Re. cynicism, you'd be cynical yourself if you were in this job. However, I am definitely leaving in abt. 3 months. Then by some time in 1944 I might be near-human again & able to write something serious. At present I'm just an orange that's been trodden on by a very dirty boots.[57]

Orwell defended himself robustly in public against the criticisms of George Woodcock, who exposed the apparent contradictions in what Orwell was doing at the BBC:

> Comrade Orwell, the former police official of British imperialism (from which the Fascists learnt all they know) in those regions of the Far East where the sun at last sets for ever on the bedraggled Union Jack! Comrade Orwell, former fellow-traveller of the pacifists and regular contributor to the pacifist *Adelphi*—which he now attacks. Comrade Orwell, former extreme left-winger, ILP partisan and defender of Anarchists (see *Homage to*

Catalonia). And now Comrade Orwell who returns to his old imperial allegiances and works for the BBC conducting British propaganda to fox the Indian masses.[58]

Privately, Orwell admitted to George Woodcock that he was being used by the governing classes, but that the defeat of nazism had to take priority over the socialist revolution.[59] Anti-fascism was the overriding cause, and Orwell's diary entry for 3 April 1942 contained a description of the writer Mulk Raj Anand which seems to echo Orwell's own conscience: 'He is genuinely anti-Fascist, and has done violence to his feelings, and probably to his reputation, by backing Britain up because he recognizes that Britain is objectively on the anti-Fascist side.'

Yet, in the Spanish Civil War, Orwell was unwilling to accept communist propaganda which, although anti-fascist, was based on the premise of winning the war before pursuing the socialist revolution. He argued that their anti-fascism was bogus but—ironically for Orwell—the cause of the popular front against fascism was ultimately fulfilled after 1941 when the United Nations fought against nazi Germany. Orwell accepted the second world war as morally necessary and this justified his participation in propaganda. But if anti-fascism was the overriding principle, why did Orwell seek, as soon as he left the BBC towards the end of 1943 when the outcome of the war was still uncertain, to write and have published a satire clearly aimed at a major anti-fascist ally? He was fully aware of the implications of what he was doing and how difficult it would be to find a publisher, but was not prepared to compromise the content, as he told T.S. Eliot:

If you read this MS yourself you will see its meaning which is not an acceptable one at the moment, but I could not agree to make any alterations except a small one at the end which I intended making anyway.[60]

If necessary, Orwell was quite prepared to have the work produced in pamphlet form, so anxious was he that it should be published. He told his literary agent Leonard Moore in July 1944: 'You understand that it is important to get this book into print & this year if possible.'[61] He had already informed Moore earlier in the year that *Animal Farm* was 'murder from the Communist point of view'[62] and that 'I particularly want this book published on political grounds'.[63] He made his political position clear in an unpublished introduction to the English edition of his book where he attacked English intellectuals for having 'swallowed and repeated Russian propaganda from 1941 onwards'.[64] In his preface to the Ukrainian edition of *Animal Farm*, Orwell told his readers that he intended to destroy the Soviet myth that Russia was a socialist country,[65] yet he made no reference to his own—albeit small—contribution to that myth in his BBC war commentaries.

This raises the important question of how relevant Orwell's experiences as a propagandist were in the fashioning of his major subsequent works. It has to be recognized that while Orwell's period at the BBC provided much useful material, it would be inaccurate to infer a simple cause and effect relationship. Orwell drew upon all his experiences for his novels and re-used that experience many times. He had long contemplated *Animal Farm* and some of the ideas in *Nineteen Eighty-Four* were anticipated even before 1941, especially in *Coming Up For Air*. Yet it is difficult to avoid the conclusion that Orwell's anxiety to publish *Animal Farm* was a particular reaction to his BBC experience and that in one sense it was a work of atonement. Orwell gave no indication of this, but it is evident that he was less concerned with commercial success than with making sure that the book reached the desired audiences. As he told his literary agent in 1947: 'I would be very glad to see a German translation of A.F. circulating in Germany and don't mind if the financial return is small.'[66] However, even earlier he had been anxious to reach an Eastern European audience. In September 1946, he was approached by Moore about a possible Serbian translation. Orwell replied: 'I have already told him [the possible translator A.G. Avakumovic] that, as in the case of other Russian-occupied countries [sic] where translations can only be made by refugees,

I don't want any payment.'[67] In January 1947, Orwell suggested to Moore the idea of smuggling copies of both Serbian and Ukrainian editions into Eastern Europe and beyond. Moreover, Orwell was fully aware of the propaganda implications of distributing such a work, in particular its likely exploitation by the right. In the case of Holland and a proposal for a serialization of *Animal Farm* in a Dutch newspaper, Orwell told his agent: 'As to the paper which is serializing it being "reactionary" I don't know that we can help that. Obviously a book of that type is liable to be made use of by Conservative Catholics etc.'[68] However, Orwell had drawn the line when a Portuguese translation was mooted. He noticed that the publishers were called *Livraria Popular de Francisco Franco*. His concern, obvious enough, was that it was linked with the Spanish dictator:

It is important to know, because I could not consider letting the firm have the book if they have any connection with the Spanish fascists. Not to put it on any other ground, it could do me a great deal of harm in this country if it got out, as it would. I know of course that Portugal itself has a semi-fascist regime and censorship of books must be pretty strict there, but that is a different matter to be definitely used as propaganda by Franco's lot.[69]

Later, when a Russian edition of *Animal Farm* was being considered, Orwell threw his scruples to the wind and approached the British Foreign Office with a view to their financing the translation, but without success.[70]

Orwell was not surprised by the use of his book as propaganda, because it was his intention that *Animal Farm* should be a work of propaganda. The irony, was of course, that it was intended to be a counter-blast to Soviet propaganda, and what more devastating portrait of a propagandist could be presented than that of Squealer, who 'could turn black into white'? As a propagandist himself, Orwell in May 1942 described the Russian workers as firmly believing that *because* their land was a socialist one, they had been able to withstand

Hitler's invasion.[71] Once his role as a propagandist was at an end, Orwell in *Animal Farm* was only too anxious to have it known that their belief was an illusion. *Animal Farm* was the product of a master propagandist who had indeed fused political and artistic purpose, and who in *Nineteen Eighty-Four* described the ultimate possibilities of state control of information in wartime. Orwell's epitaph, however, must be his own: 'It is reasonable, for example, to be willing to fight in war because one thinks the war ought to be won, and yet at the same time to refuse to write war propaganda.'[72] As a writer, Orwell had been for more than two years overwhelmed by Leviathan, but he returned to face the monster, and his own conscience.

Notes

54. 'London Letter' to *Partisan Review*, July–August 1941, *CEJL*, II, 113.

55. Ibid., 114.

56. Letter to L.F. Rushbrook-Williams, op. cit.

57. 24 August 1943, *CEJL*, II, 305.

58. 'Pacifism and the War: A Controversy', *Partisan Review*, September–October 1942, *CEJL*, II, 224.

59. Letter to George Woodcock, 2 December 1942, *CEJL*, II.

60. Letter to T.S. Eliot, 28 June 1944, *CEJL*, III, 176.

61. *CEJL*, III, 187.

62. Letter from Orwell to Moore, 19 March 1944, Lilly Library, University of Indiana.

63. Letter from Orwell to Moore, 9 May 1944, Lilly Library, University of Indiana.

64. *Times Literary Supplement*, 15 September 1972, 1038.

65. *CEJL*, III, especially 405.

66. Letter from Orwell to Moore, 8 November 1947. Henry W. and Albert A. Berg Collection. The New York Public Library. Astor, Lenox and Tilden Foundations.

67. Letter from Orwell to Moore, 21 September 1946, Berg Collection.

68. Letter from Orwell to Moore, 9 January 1947, Berg Collection.

69. Letter from Orwell to Moore, 9 November 1945. Cf. Bernard Crick, *George Orwell: A Life*: 'Because the American publication [of *Animal Farm*] was a year later than the British, Orwell was not at first aware that his book could be seen or used as anti-Socialist propaganda.' (339).

70. See Orwell's letters to Leonard Moore, 21 July 1949 and 28 July 1949. Berg Collection.

71. See footnote 48 above.

72. 'Writers and Leviathan', *Politics and Letters* (Summer 1948), *CEJL*, IV, 413.

ANTHONY KEARNEY ON THE MEANING OF EQUALITY

The famous slogan in *Animal Farm*, "All animals are equal but some are more equal than others,"[1] is more ambiguous than it has usually been taken to be. The slogan has invariably been read as meaning that some animals (the pigs) are more equal (are better) than others. If being equal is a good thing, then the more equal you are the better. This is what we might call the obvious meaning of the slogan, a meaning authorized by popular usage over half a century and so deeply embedded in everyone's mind that advertisers, among others, can use it to trigger our desire to be better than everyone else. In the novel *1984*, for obvious reasons, the phrase was used often. "Are you more equal than others?" asked *The Welding Journal*, "This is your chance to become one who is more equal than others, more expert in the welding field...."[2] Being "more equal" means excelling in certain ways and being superior to others, just as the pigs in *Animal Farm* claim to be more equal than, and superior to, the other animals.

Although not disputing that this is the obvious way to read the slogan (nearly all readers have taken it to mean just that), I suggest that in the Orwellian context of *Animal Farm*, as opposed to that outside Orwell's text, the slogan can also bear quite another meaning, one which fits even better than the obvious one the issues raised by that work. If "equal" can mean something desirable and good, it can also in a primary sense mean no more than "identical" or "same." It is this meaning, I believe, that predominates in the slogan. The slogan should read, "some animals (not the pigs) are more equal (are more the same) than others (the superior pigs)." In this reading the pigs want less equality, not more; being "more equal" means that you belong to the common herd, not the elite. In the end this may lead to much the same conclusion as in the popular reading of the slogan—the pigs in both readings are marking themselves off from the other animals—but what is at issue here is the way equality is being defined, by the pigs and of course by Orwell himself. In the obvious reading of the slogan, equality is a desirable state of affairs, with the pigs claiming more of it for themselves; in the second reading it is distinctly undesirable, and the pigs want nothing to do with it. Lower animals are equal, the higher ones decidedly unequal. The slogan allows different readings due to the exploitable ambiguities of its key term, "equal."

Orwell's own view of equality approximated that of R. H. Tawney in his classic work on the subject. For Tawney, promoting the ideal of human equality did not entail a belief in "the romantic illusion that men are equal in character and intelligence" but did entail a belief that social and economic inequalities were harmful to society.[3] In the early 1940s, at the time he was writing *Animal Farm*, Orwell also wrote approvingly of "a growing wish for greater equality" among English people, hoping that some of the worst inequalities on the social, economic, and educational fronts would be removed after the war.[4] This ideal of greater equality was obviously a basic tenet of his democratic socialism. However, his concern for the progress of equality made him extra sensitive to the unpleasant fact that the notion of equality was vulnerable to cynical manipulation by politicians. In "Politics and the English Language" (1946) Orwell lists "equality" as one of those,"words used in variable meanings, in most cases more or less dishonestly."[5] In *1984* he reveals even sharper anxieties about the term: Here not only has the ideal of equality as understood by the best political thinkers been totally abandoned, but the actual word itself has been reduced by "Newspeak" to mean no more than "identical." As Orwell phrases it in his appendix, "The Principles of Newspeak," its former associations no longer exist:

For example, All mans are equal was a possible Newspeak sentence, but only in the same sense in which All men are redhaired is a possible Old-speak sentence. It did not contain a grammatical error, but it expressed a palpable untruth—i.e. that all men are of equal size, weight, or strength. The concept of political equality no longer existed, and this secondary meaning had accordingly been purged out of the word equal.[6]

To reinforce the point, Orwell cites the passage from the American Declaration of Independence containing the phrase "all men are created equal" and adds, "It would have been quite impossible to render this into Newspeak while keeping to the sense of the original."[7]

This brutal purging of time-honored meanings of the term equality can already be seen occurring in *Animal Farm*, where the pigs themselves form an embryonic party. The pigs with their "some are more equal than others" idea begin the process—completed in the world of *1984*—whereby "equal" starts to lose its libertarian meaning and comes to mean no more than "identical." The term "equal" may, at the beginning of *Animal Farm*, hold its revolutionary connotation intact, but by the end of the book it carries a drastically reduced and sinister meaning.

If, as I think, this reading accords more convincingly than the more obvious and popular one with Orwell's main preoccupations in *Animal Farm* and *1984*, it is both ironic and appropriate that the slogan should have engendered such misreading and misapplication; it has all the appearance of a statement deliberately designed by its author to create problems of interpretation in a context where the manipulation of language is an essential part of the political process.

Notes

1. George Orwell, *Animal Farm* (Middlesex: Penguin Books, 1951) 114.

2. Qtd. in John Rodden, *The Politics of Literary Reputation: The Making and Claiming of 'St George' Orwell* (Oxford: Oxford UP, 1989) 240.

3. R. H. Tawney, *Equality* (George Allen, 1964; New York: Barnes, 1965) 57.

4. George Orwell, "The English People," *Collected Essays: Journalism and Letters of George Orwell*, vol. 3, 1943–45, eds. Sonia Orwell and Ian Angus (Middlesex: Penguin Books, 1970) 50–51.

5. George Orwell, "Politics and the English Language," *Collected Essays* vol. 4, 1946, 162.

6. George Orwell, *1984* (Middlesex: Penguin Books, 1976) 250.

7. Orwell, *1984*, 251.

MICHAEL PETERS ON *ANIMAL FARM*
50 YEARS LATER

Few books are as well-known as *Animal Farm*. Published fifty years ago, in August 1945, as the Cold War was about to begin, the novel with its mixture of simple fairy-tale and historical allegory, still has the power to charm and provoke, even though that war now seems to be part of a previous age. The novel, while frequently taught in schools to thirteen and fourteen year olds, is rarely to be found in sixth form or university syllabuses. Like the author, the book occupies an ambiguous place in the literary world. Yet its fame amongst the reading and, to an extent, the non-reading public is indisputable; the slogan, 'All animals are equal, but some are more equal than others', is one that has become part of the language.

Orwell was very clear about his intentions in writing the book. During the Spanish Civil War, he had seen the effects of the repressions and deceptions of Stalinism at first hand. He wished to open people's eyes to the reality of the Soviet regime 'in a story that could be easily understood by almost anyone', even when that regime had become an ally to Britain and the USA in the fight against German fascism. Such an exposure was essential, Orwell believed, if a true and democratic form of socialism was to be created. Working in London, first as a BBC journalist, and then as the literary editor of the *Tribune*, *Animal Farm* was written whilst the bombs dropped; one bomb even damaged the manuscript when it fell on the street where Orwell and his wife lived. Certainly the process by which the book saw the light of day was a tortuous one, with publisher after publisher finding reasons for refusing or delaying publication. For Gollancz, who had first option, and Faber, in the person of T. S. Eliot, the novel was too much of an attack on Russia, which had suffered so hugely at Stalingrad. Cape first consulted the Ministry of Information, who were concerned that the Russian leaders would take offence at their depiction as pigs, before turning the book down.

At the other end of the spectrum, even the Anarchist, Freedom Press, took exception to the novel. In America, the Dial Press thought it 'impossible to sell animal stories'. When, eventually, Warburg agreed to take the book, publication was delayed for almost a year, until the end of the European War. The question of whether this was due to a shortage of paper— the official explanation—or to political necessity, is still unresolved. From Paris, to which he travelled in February 1945, to report the War for *The Observer* at closer quarters, Orwell checked the proofs, making one last change. When the Windmill is attacked Napoleon stays standing, instead of dropping to the ground, as a tribute to Stalin's courage in remaining in Moscow during Hitler's advance; even to his enemies Orwell is determined to be fair.

Inevitably *Animal Farm*, when it was finally published, created controversy, although not of the kind originally envisaged. With the end of the struggle against fascism, a new conflict had begun to develop—the Cold War. Once effectively banned because of its politics, the book started to become an instrument of propaganda in the West's campaign to claim the moral high ground. Many new translations were produced, some with the assistance of the US State Department, and were circulated in places where Soviet influence prevailed—for example, the Ukraine and Korea. In 1947 the 'Voice of America' broadcast a radio version to Eastern Europe. The success of the novel in propaganda terms may be gauged by the Soviets' fear and loathing of the book, expressed by the seizure of copies in Germany, as well as by the cancellation of proposed radio dramatisations in Czechoslovakia. This occurred just before Soviet crackdowns in 1948 and again in 1968 on regimes which seemed to be dangerously libertarian.

Whilst Orwell was happy to see his book used to attack the Soviet myth, he did become increasingly worried about the way it was being used by the Right as a means of demonstrating that all revolutionary change was bound to fail. Picking out as central the moment when the pigs keep apples and milk for themselves, he makes the point that if 'the other animals had had the sense to put their foot down then it would have been all right'. Major's dream could have been realised. The masses should be 'alert', ready to 'chuck out their leaders as soon as they have done their job'. This is rather a different message than that found in the anti-Communist propaganda which so frequently surrounded, and surrounds, the novel.

For Orwell personally, *Animal Farm* marked his entry into the halls of literary fame. With the first impression of 4,500 copies soon sold out, sales in the UK reached 25,000 within five years, and over half a million in the US within four years. From being a marginal left-wing figure, Orwell became one of the most celebrated writers of the day, with periodic radio and television adaptations of both *Animal Farm* and *Nineteen Eighty Four*. In 1954, the first animated version of a literary text—a cartoon of *Animal Farm*—was made. However, in the last few years of his life, with a newly adopted son to bring up alone after his wife's unexpected death, and with his tuberculosis becoming increasingly serious, the success of what Orwell called his 'little squib' may have been some small comfort.

George Orwell, as many readers have done, recognised that the book's great achievement was to 'fuse political purpose and artistic purpose into one whole'. For this reason, fifty years on, in spite of the collapse of the Soviet system, in spite of the dilution of democratic socialism into liberalism, and in spite of the habit of literary critics to favour complex texts for deconstruction. *Animal Farm* may still be read with pleasure and profit, inside and outside the classroom, as one of the most imaginatively compelling satires on what Orwell called, in another of his fine phrases, the 'gramophone mind'.

In spite of its repressive features and its betrayal of basic human freedoms, then, Orwell still considered the Soviet regime to be vital as an example to the working class everywhere. The real danger lay in the idea that it defined Socialism. What was most needed was a new form of democratic Socialism created and maintained by the people. He offers meanwhile the possibility that such democratic forms of Socialism elsewhere might actually have a benign effect on the Russian regime.[27] In the allegorical context of *Animal Farm*, Napoleon's dictatorship would still seem to be a step forward from that of the human farmers—according to Orwell's letter, the rule of "the ordinary stupid capitalists." For animals outside the farm, it would provide a beacon of hope—so long as the truth about the betrayal taking place within was made plain to them. For it would now become their task to build their own movement in a democratic spirit which might, in Orwell's words, "exert a regenerative influence" on the corruption of the pigs' realm.

When *Animal Farm* finally appeared in the United States in 1946, Macdonald wrote again to Orwell, this time to discuss the book; "most of the anti-Stalinist intellectuals I know ... don't seem to share my enthusiasm for *Animal Farm*. They claim that your parable means that revolution always ends badly for the underdog, hence to hell with it and hail the status quo. My own reading of the book is that it is meant to apply to Russia without making any larger statement about the philosophy of revolution. None of the objectors have so far satisfied me when I raised this point; they admit explicitly that is all you profess to do, but still insist that implicit is the broader point.... Which view would you say comes closer to your intentions?"[28]

Orwell's reply deserves quoting in full: "Of course I intended it primarily as a satire on the Russian revolution. But I did mean it to have a wider application in so much that I meant that that kind of revolution (violent conspiratorial revolution, led by unconsciously power-hungry people) can only lead to a change of masters. I meant the moral to be that revolutions only effect a radical improvement when the masses are alert and know how to chuck out their leaders as soon as the latter have done their job. The turning point of the story was supposed to be when the pigs kept the milk and apples for themselves (Kronstadt). If the other animals had had the sense to put their foot down then, it would have been all right. If people think I am defending the status quo, that is, I think, because they have grown pessimistic and assume there is no alternative except dictatorship or laissez-faire capitalism. In the case of the Trotskyists, there is the added complication that they feel responsible for events in the USSR up to about 1926 and have to assume that a sudden degeneration took place about that date, whereas I think the whole process was foreseeable—and was foreseen by a few people, e.g. Bertrand Russell—from the very nature of the Bolshevik party. What I was trying to say was, 'You can't have a revolution unless you make it for yourself; there is no such thing as a benevolent dictatorship.'" [29]

Yes, *Animal Farm* was intended to have a wider application than a satire upon the Russian regime alone. Yes, it did indeed imply that the rule of the pigs was only "a change of masters." Yet it did not condemn to the same fate all revolutions, nor for a moment suggest that Farmer Jones should be reinstated as a more benevolent dictator than Napoleon. According to Orwell's letter, the problem examined by *Animal Farm* concerns the nature of revolution itself. Unless everyone makes the revolution for him or herself without surrendering power to an elite, there will be little hope for freedom or equality. A revolution in which violence and conspiracy become the tools most resorted to, one which is led by a consciously or unconsciously power-hungry group, will inevitably betray its own principles.[30] Failing to protest when the pigs kept the milk and apples for themselves, the other animals surrendered what power they might have had to pig leadership. Had they been "alert and [known] how to chuck out their leaders"[31] once the latter had fulfilled their task, the original spirit of Animal Farm might have been salvaged. The book itself, Orwell makes clear in his letter, was calling not for the end of revolutionary hopes, but for the beginning of a new kind of personal responsibility on the part of revolutionaries. The most important barrier in the way of such a democratic Socialist revolution was the Soviet myth: if people outside still thought that that particular form of revolution could succeed without betraying its goals, nothing new could be accomplished. The final note of Orwell's letter is optimistic: if people mistook his message for a conservative one, it was precisely their problem. They had no confidence in the possibility of an alternative to either capitalism or dictatorship. In a sense, they would be like those animals who, when forced into making a choice between a false set of alternatives by Squealer—either the return of Farmer Jones or unquestioning obedience to the rule of the pigs—failed to consider the possibility of a third choice, a democratic Socialist society. For although Orwell was prepared to provide a fairly detailed explanation of his animal story for his friend Macdonald, his letter makes it quite evident that the burden of understanding *Animal Farm* still lay with its reader.

Given the striking congruity between the text and Orwell's political commentary about it, it would be rash to argue that he had lost control of his allegory in *Animal Farm*. If it takes time and effort to expose the political intricacies behind the stark prose of his animal fable, this must have been partly his intention: the lesson of democracy was not an easy one to learn, and the next revolutionary move towards democratic Socialism could surely not be allowed to repeat the mistakes of Old Major. Still, we may wonder if the grain of hope provided by the final scene of the book is not, in this light, too insubstantial to feed a new generation of revolutionaries. Yet if Orwell had presented an easy political resolution to the horrors of totalitarianism, his warning would lose its force. His reader could remain complacent, detached from the urgent need for personal involvement in political change so emphasized by the animal allegory. If he had designed a political solution for the other beasts, furthermore, he could be accused of hypocrisy: his whole argument both inside and outside the text rested on the proposition that the people had to make and retain control of the revolution themselves if they wanted it to remain true to its goals. The deceit of the pigs was not the only failure on Animal Farm, for the foolish simplicity of the other animals and, indeed, of Old Major's naive idea of revolutionary change were as much to blame for the dictatorship which ensued. Orwell had to warn his readers that their apathy and thoughtlessness were as dangerous as blind admiration for the Stalinist regime. Only when all members of society saw the essential need for individual responsibility and honesty at the heart of any struggle for freedom and equality could the basic goals of Socialism, as Orwell saw them, be approached more closely. Meanwhile, no single revolutionary act could create a perfect world, either for the animals or for the humans whom they represent in the story. Acceptance of the notion of class struggle could not lead to an instant transformation of society unless those who would transform it accepted also the difficult burden of political power, both at the time of and after the revolution. While the most corrupting force on Animal Farm was the deception practiced upon the other animals by the pigs, the greatest danger came from the reluctance of the oppressed creatures to believe in an alternative between porcine and human rule. Yet it was in the affirmation of dignity, freedom, and equality tacitly provided by the nobler qualities of the presumed lower animals that Orwell saw the beginnings of such an alternative. So it is that, in the last moment of the book, he leaves open the task of rebuilding the revolution on a wiser and more cautiously optimistic foundation.

Notes

27. In another letter to Macdonald written at the time that Orwell was involved with his final novel, *Nineteen Eighty-Four*, he argues with an optimism which might surprise some of his critics: "Communism will presently shed certain unfortunate characteristics such as bumping off its opponents, and if Socialists join up with the CP they can persuade it into better ways" (2 May 1948, Dwight Macdonald Papers, Manuscripts and Archives, Yale University Library; copy in Orwell Archive).

28. Letter from Dwight Macdonald to Orwell, 2 December 1946, Dwight Macdonald Papers, Manuscripts and Archives, Yale

University Library; copy in Orwell Archive. The argument to which Macdonald objects is still a favorite with Orwell's critics on the Left: Stephen Sedley offers it in his critique of *Animal Farm* (Sedley, *op. cit.*).

29. Letter from Orwell to Dwight Macdonald, 5 December 1946, Dwight Macdonald Papers, Manuscripts and Archives, Yale University Library; copy in Orwell Archive. It is interesting to compare this statement with one made by Orwell in a commentary on Randall Swingler's *Violence* published in *Polemic*, V (September–October, 1946), pp. 45–53: "I do not believe in the possibility of benevolent dictatorship, nor, in the last analysis, in the honesty of those who defend dictatorship. Of course, one develops and modifies one's views, but I have never fundamentally altered my attitude towards the Soviet regime since I first began to pay attention to it some time in the nineteen-twenties. But so far from disappointing me, it has actually turned out somewhat better than I would have predicted fifteen years ago" (p. 53).

30. This is not to argue that Orwell defended pacifism; his fighting in Spain and his urgent and frequent attempts to join the army during the Second World War demonstrate his acceptance of the need for violent combat in order to defend basic human liberties. Yet he was evidently aware of the ease with which violence and conspiracy could be turned against the initial purpose which seemed to justify them. In the text of *Animal Farm*, Boxer's sorrow at the necessity of violence even in the struggle to overthrow human rule suggests a deeper wisdom than he is often given credit for (see pp. 36–7).

31 Letter from *Orwell* to Dwight Macdonald, 5 December 1946.

RICARDO QUINTANA ON ORWELL AND SATIRE

Orwell seems destined to live chiefly by his two satires. It is obvious why it was the satirist who gained a world-wide audience. Anti-totalitarianism comes closer than any other subject to being the common concern of the free world. And his treatment of this subject was brilliant—at once sensational and, by all the principles of effective satire, absolutely right. We know from his essay *Why I Write* (1947) that from 1936 onwards everything he wrote was "directly or indirectly *against* totalitarianism and *for* democratic socialism"; and that, furthermore, such writing was not spontaneous or unconsidered. On the contrary: "What I have most wanted to do ... is to make political writing into an art." Orwell criticism has in this somewhat deceptively simple statement a valid point of departure and a necessary point of arrival.

In the course of our century satire has tended to break away from its traditional forms and to merge with a species of the comic. "Existentialistic comedy" will serve as identifying term. Here the grotesque, the repulsive, and the downright horrible generate an overpowering atmosphere of bitterness and defeat. The human person is condemned to ironic insignificance. Was this the kind of satire that Orwell came to in his last phase? On the showing of *1984*, some would say yes. Yet this is to disregard *Animal Farm* and, indeed, the very nature of satire as Orwell seems to have understood it. He confessed to a profound admiration of Swift's satiric art, while at the same time repudiating everything—or almost everything—that seemed to him to constitute Swift's world view. Swift, however wrong his principles, possessed to a degree almost unequalled among prose writers the indefinable quality of style. Here was writing made into an art. The satirist who aspires to more than momentary effectiveness with his own generation must, irrespective of his principles, find a style, he must perfect an art. As novelist Orwell had taken a direction that manifestly led towards the existentialistic effect. His early naturalism had been insistent and depressing. All the experiences that were set forth ended in dysphoria. The central characters never failed to recognize themselves—certainly they consistently impressed the reader—as anti-heroes. It is to be observed, however, that Orwell never took the final step into absolute despair. These are not exactly thesis novels—he had no defined social program at the time—but his sense of injustice has a reasoned consistency that turns this consciousness into a steady point of reference. Things are evil, yes, but they hang together. This is not meaningless chaos.

It was afterwards, as I have suggested, that Orwell came to his new faith. He came to it, though, bringing with him nothing approaching the naive. He had experienced dysphoria in an acute form; it was permanently registered in his consciousness. Now he wanted something absolute, something that was not the shadow or the distortion of anything else, and he believed he had found it. But he was an inveterately nagging analyser, examining, calling in question, rejecting a good deal because it seemed phoney. He believed passionately in socialism, yet he despised most socialists and all Marxists. He was a humanist, but a completely modern one in his commitment to everlasting critical analysis. Shakespeare, he knew, had found the way to create tragic situations in which men suffer and are broken but triumph over the unknown forces that crush them. One cannot conceive of Orwell's translating his humanistic vision into any kind of tragedy, in poetry or in prose. He believed in life, but with equal conviction he believed in absolute evil—a force impossible to neutralize by emotion.

It was satire that offered him a way to keep positive and negative in balance with one another. For one like Orwell this would appear to be the only possible solution of the problem which he set for himself as writer. Is some such balance as this always effected in satire? Possibly so. If this is the case, satire stands on a somewhat different footing from both tragedy and what I have called existentialistic comedy, in both of which the pathetic—whether producing a catharsis or not—dominates. The resolution afforded by satire is a peculiar thing; it is a resolution, though neither good nor evil, death nor life, is dismissed or wholly embraced. The formal aspects of *Animal Farm* and *1984*—i.e., the precise devices brought into play and the way in which these have been manipulated—are of central importance in any study of modern satiric techniques. It is not these, however, that this discussion has been concerned with, but rather what lies behind Orwell's satiric performance. His experience both as a man and as artist has for us a sharp cogency by virtue of its entirely contemporary nature. If we come to understand his history as a writer, I believe we shall have learnt something about satire as such—something about it as a stylistic form, something about it as a psychic pattern.

Stephen Sedley on Politics and the Success of *Animal Farm*

Imaginative literature does not have to justify itself politically. On the contrary, part of its value may be to enhance or modify its readers' political comprehension. Marx's well-known preference for Balzac, a royalist, over Zola, a socialist, makes the point well enough, but it is or ought to be the experience of every socialist that it is not shared assumptions but shared experience that makes good literature a humanising and encouraging force.

Re-reading *Animal Farm* a generation after I first encountered it—as you my reader probably did—on the school curriculum, I am struck by its distance from any of these considerations. It lacks, deliberately, any effort to draw the reader into a convincing fiction, to invite a willing suspension of disbelief. Instead it demands assent to its major premise that people in their political lives can be equated with domesticated animals, and to its minor premise that civil society, like a farm, will be run for better or for worse by those who by birth or force inherit power. From these premises the story and its moral follow; without them there is neither story nor moral.

The book is still required reading in most schools ... but I was interested that my eldest child, a good reader who was given it at the age of thirteen, was bored stiff by it. The reason, it turned out, was that she was too new to political ideas to have any frame of reference for the story: she literally couldn't see what it was about. There was no invitation to enter into the fiction, no common point of departure for reader and writer.

This is certainly not a necessary condition of political allegory or satire: one has to go no farther than Orwell's next major work, *Nineteen Eighty-Four*, to see that. Nor is it a necessary condition of animal fables: our literature is rich in examples. It is an abdication of imaginative art, and one which makes the critical and pedagogic success of *Animal Farm* a sobering example of the substitution of political endorsement for critical appraisal (a vice of which the political right does not have a monopoly).

Orwell's lineage from Swift is frequently spoken of. In background and personality there are similarities, and in some of their writings too, but not in *Animal Farm*. It is not only that Swift has humour as well as passion, which Orwell does not. Swift's satirical method is practically the reverse of Orwell's. Through the picaresque fantasy of *Gulliver's Travels* or the solemn reasoning of *A Modest Proposal* Swift draws the reader down a convincing false trail. The fiction stands, as his contemporaries would have said, on its own bottom. It is only when his readers have passed the point of no return that they realise that they are reading about themselves. But you cannot get into the fiction of *Animal Farm* at all without accepting as your starting point the very thing that Orwell has to, prove—that in politics people are no better than animals: their traditional rulers may be feckless but ungovern them and a new tyranny will fill the place of the old. Naturally if you are prepared to accept that conclusion as your premise, the story follows. You can demonstrate that the earth is flat by a similar process.

(...)

Political Allegory of the Pigs

It is in the pigs that the political allegory takes its most precise form. The dream of revolution is dreamt by the old pig Major, who dies before it happens. His manifesto speech to the animals is couched in terms of self-evident absurdity:

> Man is the only real enemy we have. Remove Man from the scene, and the root cause of hunger and overwork is abolished for ever.... No argument must lead you astray. Never listen when they tell you that Man and the animals have a common interest, and that the prosperity of the one is the prosperity of the others. It is all lies.

So it is, we are to understand, with civil society: only a fool could talk like this. (The sidelight this passage throws on Orwell's brand of socialism is interesting.)

To Major's Marx, Napoleon plays Stalin and Snowball Trotsky: the allegory becomes a simple set of personal disguises. The brightest of the other animals, the dogs, are finally bribed and bred into a private army at the pigs' service. The rest, from the willing cart-horses to the fecund hens, are put upon endlessly to keep the pigs in idle comfort.

No honest socialist or communist ignores or underrates the structural and political problems and distortions which have characterised the Soviet Union and other states that have taken a similar path. 'More equal than others' is a barb which has stuck painfully in the consciousness of the left, for the existence of a privileged élite in any socialist state is a fundamental contradiction in political terms. For some on the left it argues that Marxism is not the way to socialism; for some, that Marxism has been betrayed; for some, that Marxism has been vindicated by the state's survival. Not one of these viewpoints, nor any variant of them, is explored or enriched by *Animal Farm*. Orwell's argument is pitched at a different level: it is that socialism in whatever form offers the common people no more hope than capitalism; that it will be first betrayed and then held to ransom by those forces which human beings have in common with beasts; and that the inefficient and occasionally benign rule of capitalism, which at least keeps the beasts in check, is a lesser evil. That proposition is Orwell's alpha and his omega.

So it is that the allegories of Soviet history in *Animal Farm* are just that—translations of the fall of Trotsky, the failure of the electrification program, the enforcement of collectivisation, of a ruling élite looking for scapegoats for its own errors or for other catastrophes. Nothing in the use of an animal society as the vehicle of allegory particularly illuminates or enhances it or the points it seeks to make. It certainly does not make the case against Soviet socialism any more convincing. In fact it appears to confirm the underlying hostility of its opponents to any suggestion that the working class can emancipate itself. It does nothing to cast light on what for any socialist is the real question: what has gone wrong and why? If anything it has tended to fix the left in its own errors by aversion.

Is this essay then a criticism of *Animal Farm* for what it is not, for lacking a stance which was never Orwell's anyway? It would be less than candid to deny that both its assumption that people and animals are alike in their social or political existence, and its use of that assumption to insult the belief that ordinary people can put an end to want and privilege, make *Animal Farm*, to this writer at least, a pretty unattractive book. But that is not what makes it a poor piece of literature.

PATRICK REILLY ON MITIGATING HORROR THROUGH FABLE

The very style of the fable tames catastrophe through levity, resolves terror in comedy. In life Orwell dreaded totalitarian propaganda as the supreme iniquity of our time, the throttling of truth even as a theoretic possibility; in the art of *Animal Farm* the image of a pig up a ladder with a paintbrush alchemises the horror into humour, putting Orwell and the reader in serene control of the situation. If the other animals are taken in by Squealer's impudent trickery, so much the worse for them—the reader isn't such a fool, and when he laughs at the bungled cheat he simultaneously proclaims his happy superiority to it. Material unbearable in life becomes in art a source of comic delight. When the newly liberated animals, obedient to the first duties of the victors, bring out the hams from Jones's kitchen to enact the solemn ritual of interment, the reader is invited to smile rather than mourn.

Comedy Rules

In a book where comedy rules, it is fitting that Jones should be chased off the farm with no more than a few butts and kicks, that, after his pride, his backside is the most serious casualty of the Battle of the Cowshed. Admittedly, his eventual death in alcoholic delirium is horrific enough, but it is self-inflicted, and, like the catastrophes of classical drama, occurs off-stage. The fable is inhospitable to anything resembling the ghastly conclusion in the cellar at Ekaterinburg [where the last Russian Czar and his family were murdered]—the reader would be revolted at the Joneses trampled to death under the horses' hooves or devoured by the dogs. We only hear that Jones has children because of the old discarded spelling-book which the pigs rescue from the rubbish heap in order to learn to read. In fact the Czar's children, not their primer, were flung on the rubbish heap, but the fable softens reality. Orwell insists on a victimless revolution. When, later, the men invade the farm, Orwell will not allow any of them to be killed in the successful counterattack. Boxer's massive hoof catches a stable lad on the skull, leaving him apparently "stretched ... lifeless in the mud." But here too there is the same welcome reassurance as in Shakespeare's play *The Tempest*: "Tell your piteous heart / There's no harm done."

(...)

It is crucially decisive that the tragedy happens to and among animals. The reader *knows* everything in *Animal Farm*—it is the animals who are forever mystified right up to the final bewildering metamorphosis....

Reader Is in Control

In *Animal Farm* apart from a possible irritation at being forced to choose between Napoleon and Boxer (the available options within the text are unacceptable, while the acceptable option is not available), the reader is always in control of the fable. The villain of *Animal Farm*, unlike those of *Othello* or *Nineteen Eighty-Four*, is always pellucidly open, often derisively so—we never *fear* Napoleon as we do Iago and Big Brother. The reader is in the superior position of a sophisticated onlooker at a country fair watching a bunch of yokels being taken in by a third-rate charlatan. Orwell castrates terror in the comic spectacle of an allegedly teetotal pig suffering from a hangover and swearing, like the rest of us, never to do it again. It is a scene not from the world of totalitarian terror, of Hitler and

Stalin, purges and camps, but from that of Donald McGill [a British comic] of mothers-in-law, dirty weekends and marital squabbles.

Naturally, the animals take a very different view of things, but the reader sees Napoleon less as a ferocious tyrant than as a comic cheat whose inept attempts at duplicity provoke laughter rather than indignation. When human tyrants suffer hangovers, they presumably become more fearful as the executions mount with the migraines. In Orwell's *Nineteen Eighty-Four*, we are forced to identify with Winston, the main character, and we fear Big Brother, and rightly, for our lives hang upon his whims. In *Nineteen Eighty-Four* the reader is included *in* the diminishing-technique, which makes him an insignificant bug like Winston, liable at any instant to be squashed into unpersonhood. In *Animal Farm*, by contrast, the reader is serenely above the diminution, watching with amused immunity the terrifying tale of contemporary history scaled to Lilliputian proportions, tamed to the level of barnyard fable. The prophecy magnifies the tyrant and diminishes the reader; the allegory magnifies the reader and diminishes the tyrant.

Orwell knew from personal experience how thoroughly dislikable pigs could be. He wrote in a letter: "The pig has grown to a stupendous size and goes to the butcher next week. We are all longing to get rid of him, as he is so destructive and greedy, even gets into the kitchen at times." In life the troublesome pig goes to the butcher; in the nightmare fairy tale the pig decides who goes to the butcher and is not just occasionally in the kitchen but in unchallengeable control of the house itself. But the trivialisation implicit in the fable form necessarily keeps the reader superior and secure.

All the events are deliberately diminished. The suppression of the kulaks in the Ukraine is reduced to a rebellion of hens at the sale of their eggs; it ends with nine hens starved to death— the fable's equivalent of the millions of peasants who died in the aftermath of Stalin's victory. Swift in Lilliput similarly trivialises the wars of the Reformation to an absurd wrangle between Big- and Little-Endians. Orwell employs the same technique to exchange the harrowing emotions provoked by twentieth-century history for an Olympian pose, so making the events easier to handle. The allegations of industrial sabotage which issued in the Moscow showcase trials dwindle into a broken window and a blocked drain, while treason to the Revolution finds its appropriate image in a sheep urinating in a drinking-pool.

The most amusingly "domestic" of these substitutions is the account of Mollie's defection. We hear that she is becoming "more and more troublesome," and there are rumors of "something more serious" than her habitual giddiness. What Marxist and social philosopher Herbert Marcuse deplores as the seduction of large sections of the Western working class, bribed by the titbits of consumerism, is here depicted in terms of a fallen woman of Victorian melodrama, as Mollie goes down the well-worn road of Little Em'ly and Hetty Sorrel. The matronly Clover does her best to save the wanton—she is accepting sugar and ribbons from the men, has even been caught *in flagrante delicto* allowing her nose to be stroked—but the attempted rescue is as futile as Mrs Poyser's remonstrations. The last the scandalised animals hear is that Mollie is traipsing about town with a vulgar publican; after this, "none of the animals ever mentioned Mollie again." The shame of the lapse is emphasized in the best Victorian tradition. When the animals metaphorically turn Mollie's face to the wall, the reader applauds the reductive wit, and, in his amusement, necessarily neglects the seriousness of the defection as viewed from Marcuse's perspective....

Orwell's purpose is to control a material which, taken at its everyday estimate and customary magnification, would cause the writer pain, alarm and indignation. Small is masterable; when Stalin becomes a pig and Europe a farmyard, the nightmare of contemporary history is transmuted, through the power of art, into a blithe and inspired fantasy.

Thus to criticise Orwell for allegedly demeaning the common people by depicting them as moronically credulous brutes is to misread the book. The animal fable is devised not to insult the ordinary man but to distance Orwell from the terror: existence becomes endurable as an aesthetic phenomenon. Philosopher Schiller argues that only in art is man free. German novelist Thomas Mann described his Joseph tetralogy [a series of books], written between 1926 and 1943 (the period covered by Orwell's fable), as his attempt to escape the horror by burying himself in an innocent and serene creation of the Spirit. Simplicity is an essential part of Orwell's disarming strategy. *Animal Farm*, as its subtitle "A Fairy Tale" makes plain, is a convenient simplification, yet its simplicity came hard: "the only one of my books I really sweated over," he wrote. Orwell's efforts were fully justified....

CHRISTOPHER HOLLIS ON *ANIMAL FARM'S* LITERARY MERIT

The interpretation of the fable is plain enough. Major, Napoleon, Snowball—Lenin, Stalin and Trotsky—Pilkington and Frederick, the two groups of non-Communist powers—the Marxian thesis, as expounded by Major, that society is divided into exploiters and exploited and that all the exploited need to do is to rise up, to expel the exploiters and seize the 'surplus value' which the exploiters have previously annexed to, themselves—the Actonian thesis that power corrupts and the Burnhamian thesis that the leaders of the exploited, having used the rhetoric of equality to get rid of the old exploiters, establish in their place not a classless society but themselves as a new governing class—the greed and unprincipled opportunism of the non-Communist states, which are ready enough to overthrow the Communists by force so long as they imagine that their overthrow will be easy but begin to talk of peace when they find the task difficult and when they think that they can use the Communists to satisfy their greed—the dishonour among total thugs, as a result of which, though greed may make original ideology irrelevant, turning pigs into men and men into pigs, the thugs fall out among themselves, as the Nazis and the Communists fell out, not through difference of ideology but because in a society of utter baseness and insincerity there is no motive of confidence. The interpretation is so plain that no serious critic can dispute it. Those Russian critics who have professed to see in it merely a general satire on bureaucracy without any special reference to any particular country can hardly be taken seriously.

Yet even a total acceptance of Orwell's political opinions would not in itself make *Animal Farm* a great work of art. The world is full of animal fables in which this or that country is symbolized by this or that animal, and very tedious affairs the greater number of them are—and that, irrespective of whether we agree or disagree with their opinions. To be a great book, a book of animal fables requires literary greatness as well as a good cause. Such greatness *Animal Farm* surely possesses. As Orwell fairly claimed, *Animal Farm* 'was the first book in which I tried, with full consciousness of what I was doing, to fuse political purpose and artistic purpose into one whole'—and he succeeded.

The problems that are set by this peculiar form of art, which makes animals behave like human beings, are clear. The writer must throughout be successful in preserving a delicate and whimsical balance. As Johnson truly says in his criticism of Dryden's *Hind and the Panther*, there is an initial absurdity in making animals discuss complicated intellectual problems—the nature of the Church's authority in Dryden's case, the communist ideology in Orwell's. The absurdity can only be saved from ridicule if the author is able to couch his argument in very simple terms and to draw his illustrations from the facts of animal life. In this Orwell is as successful as he could be—a great deal more successful incidentally than Dryden, who in the excitement of the argument often forgets that it is animals who are supposed to be putting it forward. The practical difficulties of the conceit must either be ignored or apparently solved in some simple and striking—if possible, amusing—fashion. Since obviously they could not in reality be solved at all, the author merely makes himself ridiculous if he allows himself to get bogged down in tedious and detailed explanations which at the end of all cannot in the nature of things explain anything. Thus Orwell is quite right merely to ignore the difficulties of language, to assume that the animals can communicate with one another by speech—or to assume that the new ordinance which forbids any animal to take another animal's life could be applied with only the comparatively mild consequence of gradual increase in animal population. He is justified in telling us the stories of the two attacks by men for the recapture of the Farm but in refusing to spoil his story by allowing the men to take the full measures which obviously men would take if they found themselves in such an impossible situation. The means by which the animals rout the men are inevitably signally unconvincing if we are to consider them seriously at all. It would as obviously be ridiculous to delay for pages to describe how animals build windmills or how they write up commandments on a wall. It heightens the comedy to give a passing sentence of description to their hauling the stone up a hill so that it may be broken into manageable fractions when it falls over the precipice, or to Squealer, climbing a ladder to paint up his message.

Works by George Orwell

Down and Out in Paris and London, 1933.
Burmese Days: A Novel, 1934.
A Clergyman's Daughter, 1935.
Keep the Aspidistra Flying, 1936.
The Road to Wigan Pier, 1937.
Homage to Catalonia, 1938.
Coming Up for Air, 1939.
The Lion and the Unicorn: Socialism and the English Genius, 1941.
Animal Farm: A Fairy Story, 1945.
Nineteen Eighty-Four: A Novel, 1949.

Annotated Bibliography

Alldritt, Keith. *The Making of George Orwell: An Essay in Literary History*. New York: St. Martin's Press, 1961.

Written by a Professor of English at the University of British Columbia, this work traces Orwell's literary development from his rebellion against the Symbolist tradition to the "deeper and less easily defined forces at work" behind his undertaking of the "George Orwell" persona.

Calder, Jenni. *Chronicles of Conscience: A Study of George Orwell and Arthur Koestler*. London: Secker & Warburg, 1968.

A comparative study of the work of both writers, this places Orwell in a wider European context, evoking the work of Sartre, Jack London, H.G. Wells, and Arnold Zweig, among others. Calder concludes that Orwell's work will remain relevant so long as authoritarian regimes continue to exist.

Gross, Miriam. *The World of George Orwell*. London: Weidenfeld & Nicholson, 1971.

In the introduction to this illustrated compendium of essays, Gross writes that she tries to see Orwell "both in terms of what he means today and as a man whose achievement very much needs to be set in the context of his own period."

Hitchens, Christopher. *Why Orwell Matters*. New York: Basic Books, 2002.

A contributor to *The Nation* and *Vanity Fair* describes Orwell's prescience about the "three great subjects of the twentieth century:" imperialism, fascism, and Stalinism. Also features description and analysis of Orwell's time in Burma and Spain.

Hollis, Christopher. *A Study of George Orwell*. London: Hollis and Carter, 1956.

One of the first substantive studies of Orwell, this was

written by an Eton classmate and contemporary who visited him in Burma in 1925.

Kubal, David. *Outside the Whale: George Orwell's Art and Politics.* Notre Dame: University of Notre Dame Press, 1972.

This study explores the connection between Orwell's political ideology and his art. Kubal argues that Orwell felt he had to sacrifice his responsibility as an artist for his political and moral obligations.

Meyers, Jeffrey. *Orwell: Wintry Conscience of a Generation.* New York: W.W. Norton, 2000.

This biography paints a dark portrait of the writer by including new research and unpublished anecdotes from Orwell's family and close friends. Meyers draws on a close study of Orwell's *Complete Works* and delves into new material from the Orwell Archive in London.

Orwell, Sonia, and Ian Angus IV, eds. *The Collected Essays, Journalism, and Letters of George Orwell.* London: Secker & Warburg, 1968.

These four volumes cover the years 1920 to 1950. In addition to a comprehensive collection of letters, this book also features the longer essays—such as "Shooting an Elephant" and "Dickens, Dali, and Others"—which have been featured in other collections, as well as some of the *Collected Essays*, which were published posthumously in 1961.

Reilly, Patrick. *George Orwell: The Age's Adversary.* New York: St. Martin's Press, 1986.

This study suggests that Orwell's work is a relevant tool for solving the political problems of today. Reilly, who has also written extensively on Swift, one of Orwell's heroes, explains the sentiments and motivation behind such Orwell statements as "It is not possible for any thinking person to live in such a society as our own without wanting to change it."

Rodden, John. *The Politics of Literary Reputation: The Making and Claiming of "St. George" Orwell.* Oxford: Oxford University Press, 1989.

This work maps out the writer's four dominant images: the rebel, the common man, the prophet, and the saint. Rodden also analyzes Orwell's critical reception by isolating the viewpoint of the critic and exploring how such a stance reflects the U.S. political climate.

Stansky, Peter, and William Abrahams. *The Transformation.* London: Constable and Company Limited, 1979.

This biography, the sequel to *The Unknown Orwell,* covers four crucial years in the life of the burgeoning novelist and social critic. Drawing on Orwell's work and interviews, the authors describe the publication of *Down and Out in Paris and London* and the quick succession of three subsequent works.

Taylor, D.J. *Orwell: The Life.* New York: Henry Holt & Co., 2003.

This biography analyzes Orwell's work and pays equal if not greater attention to the author's hold on his image, suggesting that his goals and his writing were often at odds with his life.

Trilling, Lionel. "George Orwell and the Politics of Truth." From *The Moral Obligation to Be Intelligent: Selected Essays.* New York: Farrar, Straus & Giroux, 2000.

This essay, written on the occasion of the U.S. publication of *Homage to Catalonia,* describes Orwell as a truth teller and explains why his disparagement of those liberals who "refused to understand the conditioned nature of life" cost him friends. Jeffrey Meyers has called this "probably the most influential essay on Orwell."

Williams, Raymond. *George Orwell: A Collection of Critical Essays.* Englewood Cliffs, New Jersey: Prentice-Hall, 1974.

This collection spans three generations of Orwell criticism.

Writers include Terry Eagleton, Richard Hoggart, Lionel Trilling, E.P. Thompson, John Wain, Jenni Calder, and George Woodcock.

Woodcock, George. *The Crystal Spirit: A Study of George Orwell*. Boston: Little, Brown, 1966.

One of the most influential works on Orwell, it studies the diverse elements that make up Orwell's personality.

Zwerdling, Alex. *Orwell and the Left*. New Haven: Yale University Press, 1974.

Analyzes Orwell's relationship to Marxism and other left-wing ideals—describes him as a critic of socialism—and views his art through this lens.

Contributors

Harold Bloom is Sterling Professor of the Humanities at Yale University. He is the author of 30 books, including *Shelley's Mythmaking* (1959), *The Visionary Company* (1961), *Blake's Apocalypse* (1963), *Yeats* (1970), *A Map of Misreading* (1975), *Kabbalah and Criticism* (1975), *Agon: Toward a Theory of Revisionism* (1982), *The American Religion* (1992), *The Western Canon* (1994), and *Omens of Millennium: The Gnosis of Angels, Dreams, and Resurrection* (1996). *The Anxiety of Influence* (1973) sets forth Professor Bloom's provocative theory of the literary relationships between the great writers and their predecessors. His most recent books include *Shakespeare: The Invention of the Human* (1998), a 1998 National Book Award finalist, *How to Read and Why* (2000), *Genius: A Mosaic of One Hundred Exemplary Creative Minds* (2002), *Hamlet: Poem Unlimited* (2003), *Where Shall Wisdom be Found* (2004), and *Jesus and Yahweh: The Names Divine* (2005). In 1999, Professor Bloom received the prestigious American Academy of Arts and Letters Gold Medal for Criticism. He has also received the International Prize of Catalonia, the Alfonso Reyes Prize of Mexico, and the Hans Christian Andersen Bicentennial Prize of Denmark.

Sarah Robbins holds an MFA in fiction writing from New School University. She is a New York City–based writer and editor. Her nonfiction has appeared in publications including the *American Book Review*, *ArtNews*, *Glamour*, and *Newsday*, and she is currently at work on a novel.

Edward Crankshaw won the Whitbread Book Award for *Bismarck* in 1982. He is also the author of *Maria Theresa* (1970) and *The Hapsburgs* (1971).

Matthew Hodgart was a Fellow of Pembroke College, Cambridge University, and the coauthor of *Joyce's Grand*

Operoar: Opera in Finnegan's Wake (1996) and author of *James Joyce: A Student's Guide* (1978).

Raymond Williams was one of the earliest cultural theorists and a lecturer at Oxford University. He is the author of *Culture and Society 1780-1950* (1958) and *The Long Revolution* (1961).

Graham Greene is the author of *The Power and the Glory* (1940), *The End of the Affair* (1951), and *The Quiet American* (1955), among others.

Kingsley Martin was the editor of *The New Statesman* and author of *The Triumph of Lord Palmerston* (1924), *French Liberal Thought in the Eighteenth Century* (1929), and two autobiographical works, *Father Figures* (1966) and *Editor* (1968).

Cyril Connolly was an English critic and novelist. He was the editor of *Horizon* magazine, a frequent contributor to the Sunday *Times*, and the author of *Enemies of Promise* (1948) and *The Unquiet Grave* (1945).

Isaac Rosenfeld wrote for magazines including *The New Republic, The Nation, Partisan Review,* and *Commentary*. He is the author of *Alpha and Omega* (1966) and *Passage from Home* (1988).

Edmund Wilson was a celebrated author and critic. He was an editor at the *New Republic* and a book reviewer at the *New Yorker*.

Northrop Frye was Professor of English at the University of Toronto. He is the author of *Anatomy of Criticism* (1957), *The Educated Imagination* (1963), *The Bush Garden* (1971), *The Great Code* (1982), and *Words with Power* (1990), among others. He won the Governor General's Literary Award for non-Fiction for his book *Northrop Frye on Shakespeare* (1986).

Robert Pearce was a Professor of History at the University College of St. Martin, Lancaster, and a Fellow of the Royal Historical Society. The author of a dozen history books, he has also edited and introduced six volumes in the Duckworth 'Sayings' series.

C. Fleay and **M.L. Sanders** have also collaborated in *Historical Journal*: "The Labour Spain Committee: Labour Party Policy and The Spanish Civil War."

Anthony Kearney taught at La Trobe University, Australia, and at St. Martin's College, England. He has published several pieces in *Victorian Poetry* as well as a book on John Churton Collins.

Michael Peters is the editor of *Education and the Postmodern Condition*, with a foreword by Jean-Francois Lyotard (1995), and author of *Poststructuralism, Politics, and Education* (1996).

V.C. Letemendia is an Adjunct Professor in the Department of Political Science, University of Toronto. Her field of interest is the relationship between politics and literature. She is also the author of "Poverty in the Writings of Albert Camus."

Ricardo Quintana is the author of *Eighteenth Century Plays* (1966) and *The Mind and Art of Jonathan Swift* (1965).

Stephen Sedley is a Lord Justice of Appeal and has sat as the U.K. judge in the European Court of Human Rights.

Patrick Reilly is the author of many books, including *Jonathan Swift: The Brave Desponder* (1982), *Nineteen Eighty-Four: Past, Present, and Future* (1989), and *Lord of the Flies: Fathers and Sons* (1992).

Christopher Hollis was educated at Balliol College and Eton, where he was a classmate of Orwell's. He is the author of *Erasmus* (1933), *The Mind of Chesterton* (1970), and *Oxford in the Twenties* (1976).

Acknowledgments

From "Orwell and Communism" by Edward Crankshaw, in *The World of George Orwell*, edited by Miriam Gross. pp. 118–126.© 1971 George Weidenfeld and Nicolson, Ltd. Reprinted by Permission

From "Animal Farm to Nineteen Eighty-Four" by Matthew Hodgart in *The World of George Orwell*, edited by Miriam Gross. pp. 137–139. © 1971 George Weidenfeld and Nicolson Ltd. Reprinted by permission.

From *George Orwell* by Raymond Williams. pp. 71–75. Copyright © 1971 by Raymond Williams. Used by permission of Viking Penguin, a division of Penguin Group (USA) Inc.

Selections from *George Orwell: The Critical Heritage*, edited by Jeffrey Meyers. pp. 195–208. © 1975 Routledge & Kegan Paul. Reproduced by permission of Taylor and Francis Books UK.

Robert Pearce, "Orwell, Tolstoy, and Animal Farm", *The Review of English Studies*, New Series, Vol. 49, No. 193 (Feb. 1998), pp. 66–68. © 1998 Oxford University Press. Reprinted by permission

"Looking in to the Abyss: George Orwell at the BBC", by C. Fleay and M.L. Sanders, in *Journal of Contemporary History*, Vol. 24, No. 3 (Jul. 1989), pp. 512–515. ©1989 Sage Publications. Used by permission of Sage Publications Ltd.

"Orwell's Animal Farm and 1984," *Explicator*, Summer 1996, Vol. 54, Issue 4, p. 238–240. Reprinted by permission of the Helen Dwight Reid Educational Foundation. Published by Heldref Publications, 1319 Eighteenth St., NW, Washington, DC 20036-1802. Copyright © 1996.

Index

Characters in literary works are indexed by first name (if any), followed by the name of the work in parentheses